الاستنباط من البحر العميق

AL- ISTINBĀTU MIN AL BAHRI AL A'MÌQ

DROPS FROM THE DEEP OCEAN

REFLECTIONS ON THE QUR'AN

Tazkiyah and Layyinah as The Prophetic Atmosphere

with a focus on

- ► Contemporary Renderings
- ► Psychological Explorations
- ► Western Discourses
- ► Lexical Analysis

VOLUME 7

Dr. M. Yunus Kumek

Address to the Islamic Religious Scholars & Philosophers

Cover Photo by Y. Kumek, Alexandria, Egypt, January 12, 2019.

Medina Houseᶜ
publishing

www.medinahouse.org
170 Manhattan Ave, Po. Box 63
New York 14215
contact@medinahouse.org

Published in the United States of America.

TABLE OF CONTENTS

VOLUME 7

بِسْمِ اللّٰهِ الرَّحْمَنِ الرَّحِيمِ[1]

الْحَمْدُ لِلّٰهِ رَبِّ الْعَالَمِينَ[2]
اللّٰهُمَّ صَلِّ عَلَى سَيِّدِنَا وَ حَبِيْبَنَا وَ مَوْلَنَا مُحَمَّد[3]

Preface

Different Styles of the Qurãn

When we look at the Qurãn in its style and content, one can realize some of the distinctive perspectives as follows.

The Inclusivity of the Qurãn for Different Stakeholders

When the ayahs of the Qurãn are analyzed by the different experts in different fields, a phrase can have different meanings for each expertise of specialty.

For example, if we analyze the ayah[4] {النبأ/7} وَالْجِبَالَ أَوْتَادًا, a regular ordinary person can have some understanding. At the same time, geographer, a poet, and a geophysicist can understand and deduce different meanings from the same simple looking phrase. Yet, none of them find it contradicting in their field of this study with this description.

Even, a scholar or a specialist with imãn, who knows fully and absolutely that the Qurãn is from Rabbul Alamìn, he or she centers the Qurãn to receive inspirations for different discoveries in their disciplines of scientific expertise. One can remember the golden age of Islãm with different scientific discoveries and innovations as inspired with Islamic teachings [1].

---

1. In the name of Allah, the Entirely Merciful, the Especially Merciful.
2. [All] praise is [due] to Allah, Lord of the worlds.
3. O Allah, bless our master, our beloved, and Mawlana Muhammed (PBUH).
4. And the mountains as stakes?

أَوَلَمْ يَرَ الَّذِينَ كَفَرُوا أَنَّ السَّمَاوَاتِ وَالْأَرْضَ كَانَتَا Here is another example as [5] رَتْقًا فَفَتَقْنَاهُمَا وَجَعَلْنَا مِنَ الْمَاء كُلَّ شَيْءٍ حَيٍّ أَفَلَا يُؤْمِنُونَ {الأنبياء/30}. If an ordinary person fifteen centuries ago analyzes this ayah, he or she may realize that there is an information that is presented here something very new and not usual about the first creation of universe. As we travel in the timeline of the history, this has not been fully understood until with the recent scientific advancements. Until this time, Muslims with adab believed and submitted what Allah ﷻ has mentioned in the Qurān. Possibly, some non-Muslims did not understand this unusual and new information about the creation of the universe and they made mockery about the Qurān.

Yet, today's big bang theory states that [1]

the rapid expansion of matter from a state of extremely high density and temperature that according to current cosmological theories marked the origin of the universe.

A fireball of radiation at extremely high temperature and density, but occupying a tiny volume, is believed to have formed around 13.7 billion years ago. This expanded and cooled, extremely fast at first, but more slowly as subatomic particles condensed into matter that later accumulated to form galaxies and stars.

Above knowledge of big bang theory has become today an ordinary information presented in middle/high school textbooks. Yet, this was seen as an unusual for a person fifteen centuries ago.

On the other hand, within these current scientific advances, there are still a lot of unknowns about the big bang theory althouth it is in line with the explicit information of the ayah as [6] أَوَلَمْ يَرَ الَّذِينَ كَفَرُوا أَنَّ السَّمَاوَاتِ وَالْأَرْضَ كَانَتَا رَتْقًا فَفَتَقْنَاهُمَا وَجَعَلْنَا مِنَ الْمَاء كُلَّ شَيْءٍ حَيٍّ أَفَلَا يُؤْمِنُونَ {الأنبياء/30}.

Yet, when an astrophysicist analyzes the above ayah, he or she can have an access to an information that is not available today in the details of big bang theory.

---

5. Have those who disbelieved not considered that the heavens and the earth were a joined entity, and We separated them and made from water every living thing? Then will they not believe?

6. Have those who disbelieved not considered that the heavens and the earth were a joined entity, and We separated them and made from water every living thing? Then will they not believe?

This shows the inclusivity of the Qurãn at all times for different experts, scholars and scientists.

The Birth of Different Sciences with the Qurãn

When one analyzes Islamic scholarship, there are different sciences that emerged due to different openings of the Qurãn for the establishment of new disciplines. Some of them are fiqh-legal rulings, tafsìr-exegesis, kalãm (reason/philosophy in belief), tasawwuf-spiritual sciences, ahlãq-ethics & morality.

After birth of these above sciences, there has been a meticulous methodology developed ensuring critical thinking and experience, authenticity, verification/confirmation, transmission of the knowledge resulting to establish very methodological golden guidelines.

It is accepted by both Christian and Jewish scholars that these methodological golden guidelines affected and helped to develop and substantiate the methodological principles of Christianity through Thomas Aquinas and Judaism through Maimanes [3]. Especially, when there was a warm and peaceful interaction between different religious groups in Andalucía, the intellectual influence of Islamic scholarship was very vivid through Imam Ghazali, Ibn Sina, and others [3].

VOLUME 7

Sûrah 2 – al-Baqara

[26-27][7]

إِنَّ اللَّهَ لاَ يَسْتَحْيِي أَن يَضْرِبَ مَثَلاً مَّا بَعُوضَةً فَمَا فَوْقَهَا فَأَمَّا الَّذِينَ آمَنُواْ فَيَعْلَمُونَ أَنَّهُ الْحَقُّ مِن رَّبِّهِمْ وَأَمَّا الَّذِينَ كَفَرُواْ فَيَقُولُونَ مَاذَا أَرَادَ اللَّهُ بِهَذَا مَثَلاً يُضِلُّ بِهِ كَثِيراً وَيَهْدِي بِهِ كَثِيراً وَمَا يُضِلُّ بِهِ إِلاَّ الْفَاسِقِينَ {البقرة/26} الَّذِينَ يَنقُضُونَ عَهْدَ اللَّهِ مِن بَعْدِ مِيثَاقِهِ وَيَقْطَعُونَ مَا أَمَرَ اللَّهُ بِهِ أَن يُوصَلَ وَيُفْسِدُونَ فِي الأَرْضِ أُولَئِكَ هُمُ الْخَاسِرُونَ {البقرة/27}

The process of formation of doubts

The lower nafs can always tend to approach the teachings and examples of the Qurãn with the darkness of the kufr, disbelief. Accordingly, it does not understand the hikmah, wisdom of these examples. Due to the tendency of the spiritual sickness in the heart, any doubt or question can become so important and so critical as if, they become the essence and pillar of the religion. Then, naturally, the person loses the right path, al-haqq as invaded with the doubts in the heart and mind. Then, this person starts asking questions. Still, he or she cannot find solution to his or her doubts. Then, he or she starts denial, disbelief, unappreciation, ungratefulness of pessimism and darkness referred as kufr.

After the above internal dark, pessimistic and destructive psychological journey of kufr, above ayah mentions the display of the question as مَاذَا أَرَادَ اللَّهُ بِهَذَا مَثَلاً.

May Allah ﷻ protect us, Amìn.

Humbleness, humility, tawãdu, always but always reliance to Allah ﷻ with tawakkul are the key elements to be safe as life vest. When the person trusts in himself or herself even for a size of atom, then this can for sure be the point of loss and turning point to darkness and pessimism. The real power, light, calmness, serenity, peace and tranquility is in full

---

7. Indeed, Allah is not timid to present an example—that of a mosquito or what is smaller than it. And those who have believed know that it is the truth from their Lord. But as for those who disbelieve, they say, "What did Allah intend by this as an example?" He misleads many thereby and guides many thereby. And He misleads not except the defiantly disobedient,

and all trust to Allah ﷻ. Therefore, the dua of Rasulullah ﷺ as "wa la takilni tarfata 'aynun, oh Allah!, do not leave me by trusting in my own self even less than blinking of an eye, Amìn," can show this real, absolute, and required disposition of a mu'min, believer.

Allahumma Ja'alna minhum, Amìn!

اللَّهُمَّ جَعَلْنَا مِنهُم ، آمين

Attitudes Leading to Imān or Kufr

When we analyze the portion of the ayah as فَأَمَّا الَّذِينَ آمَنُواْ فَيَعْلَمُونَ أَنَّهُ الْحَقُّ مِن رَّبِّهِمْ وَأَمَّا الَّذِينَ كَفَرُواْ فَيَقُولُونَ مَاذَا أَرَادَ اللّهُ بِهَذَا مَثَلاً, there are very critical elements that emerge in this simple looking but very convoluted statement.

The symmetry in balagah can indicate the opposite of فَأَمَّا الَّذِينَ آمَنُواْ لا يعلمون ... وَأَمَّا الَّذِينَ كَفَرُوا to be فَيَعْلَمُونَ أَنَّهُ الْحَقُّ مِن رَّبِّهِمْ. Yet, the response of the people of kufr is فَيَقُولُونَ مَاذَا أَرَادَ اللَّهُ بِهَذَا مَثَلاً.

This can indicate that the attitude is the final and ultimate cause and reason of one's hidayah, guidance, leading to imān or misguidance, leading to kufr. May Allah ﷻ protect us, Amìn!

This reality of guidance and misguidance is mentioned immediately in the same ayah as يُضِلُّ بِهِ كَثِيراً وَيَهْدِي بِهِ كَثِيراً.

In this external sense, yes, Allah ﷻ can guide and misguide any person. Yet, one should really look into the causes of this final statement of يُضِلُّ بِهِ كَثِيراً وَيَهْدِي بِهِ كَثِيراً. In other words, guidance is with the Rahmah, Fadl and Grace of Allah ﷻ due to showing inclinations of humbleness and humility on the path of Allah ﷻ.

Misguidance, dalalah and ending up in kufr is the attitude of kufr and fisq as mentioned in {البقرة/62}وَمَا يُضِلُّ بِهِ إلاَّ الْفَاسِقِينَ. In this sense, the expression [8] وَمَا يُضِلُّ بِهِ إلاَّ الْفَاسِقِينَ {البقرة/62} shuts off and slams the anyone immediately who has a miniscule or atom size tendency even in their thoughts or emotions to blame Allah ﷻ, astagfirullah, SubhanAllah, for the misguidance. Furthermore, the expressions و and مَا and بِهِ and إلاَّ and the ma'rifah, definite form in الْفَاسِقِينَ and the mudari form indicating the result of kasb but not the qada as would be indicated with madi in يُضِلُّ all strongly and definitely emphasize, underline and stress the

---

8. Indeed, Allah is not timid to present an example—that of a mosquito or what is smaller than it. And those who have believed know that it is the truth from their Lord. But as for those who disbelieve, they say, "What did Allah intend by this as an example?" He misleads many thereby and guides many thereby. And He misleads not except the defiantly disobedient,

specificity, hāss, with ta'kid that there is a specific group, and a specific reason. Therefore, due to their kasb, acquisition, they end up in kufr and misguidance with their choice. May Allah ﷻ protect us.

If we further analyze the expression other diamonds and pearls can reveal themselves with the Fadl, Grace and Tawfik of Allah ﷻ to support this disposition.

For example, in the part فَأَمَّا الَّذِينَ آمَنُواْ فَيَعْلَمُونَ أَنَّهُ الْحَقُّ مِن رَّبِّهِمْ, the people of imān do not claim that they understood fully the example of بَعُوضَةَ, the fly or mosquito. Yet, the attitude of imān necessitates humbleness and humility of submission that whatever Allah ﷻ mentions, they know that that is the truth, al-haqq as mentioned فَيَعْلَمُونَ أَنَّهُ الْحَقُّ. They may try to understand the hikmah, and wisdom in these teachings to increase their yaqìn, certainty about marifatullah. Yet, their initial attitude is not to object, to question, or implicitly make fun like a kāfir or munāfiq.

When one analyzes the responses of the kāfir or munāfiqs in the Qurān, one can realize this initial and immediate position of objection, questioning, and arrogance as their display of kufr and nifāq in misguidance. For example, [9] وَيَقُولُونَ سَمِعْنَا وَعَصَيْنَا وَاسْمَعْ غَيْرَ مُسْمَعٍ وَرَاعِنَا لَيًّا بِأَلْسِنَتِهِمْ وَطَعْنًا فِي الدِّينِ وَلَوْ أَنَّهُمْ قَالُواْ سَمِعْنَا وَأَطَعْنَا وَاسْمَعْ وَانظُرْنَا لَكَانَ خَيْرًا لَّهُمْ وَأَقْوَمَ وَلَكِن لَّعَنَهُمُ اللّهُ بِكُفْرِهِمْ فَلاَ يُؤْمِنُونَ إِلاَّ قَلِيلاً {النساء/46}

The primary example of this Shaytān when he was ordered to make sajdah to Adam as, he did not fulfill it but questioned. Then, in this attitude his followers follow Shaytān from ins and jinn. The statement مَاذَا أَرَادَ اللّهُ بِهَذَا مَثَلاً is one of the examples of the same group of followers.

Oppositely, the people of imān has the initial and immediate position of humbleness and humility for any teaching coming from Allah ﷻ with acceptance, submission and following. For example, [10] وَإِذَا سَمِعُواْ مَا أُنزِلَ إِلَى الرَّسُولِ تَرَى أَعْيُنَهُمْ تَفِيضُ مِنَ الدَّمْعِ مِمَّا عَرَفُواْ مِنَ الْحَقِّ يَقُولُونَ رَبَّنَا آمَنَّا فَاكْتُبْنَا مَعَ الشَّاهِدِينَ {المائدة/38}

رَبَّنَا آمَنَّا بِمَا أَنزَلَتْ وَاتَّبَعْنَا الرَّسُولَ فَاكْتُبْنَا مَعَ الشَّاهِدِينَ {آل عمران/53}

---

9. Among the Jews are those who distort words from their [proper] usages and say, "We hear and disobey" and "Hear but be not heard" and "Ra'ina," twisting their tongues and defaming the religion. And if they had said [instead], "We hear and obey" and "Wait for us [to understand]," it would have been better for them and more suitable. But Allah has cursed them for their disbelief, so they believe not, except for a few.

10. And when they hear what has been revealed to the Messenger, you see their eyes overflowing with tears because of what they have recognized of the truth. They say, "Our Lord, we have believed, so register us among the witnesses.

وَقَالُوا۟ سَمِعْنَا وَأَطَعْنَا غُفْرَانَكَ رَبَّنَا وَإِلَيْكَ الْمَصِيرُ [11] {البقرة/285}

The primary examples of this is angels when ordered to make sajdah for Adam as. They fulfilled the ordered although they had a question with adab to Allah ﷻ about the creation of Adam as.

If we analyze further the expression فَأَمَّا الَّذِينَ آمَنُوا۟ فَيَعْلَمُونَ أَنَّهُ الْحَقُّ مِن رَّبِّهِمْ , the choice of Attribute and Name of Allah ﷻ as رَّبِّهِمْ show the intrinsic disposition of proximity, sincerity, and humbleness and humility of the people of imān in their heart and mind in actualizing the commands and teachings of Allah ﷻ.

On the other hand, the statement of usage the Dhāt as اللّٰه of the people of kufr or nifāq in the expression مَاذَا أَرَادَ اللّٰهُ بِهَٰذَا مَثَلاً can indicate their distance, fake and arrogant dispositions from Rabbul Alamìn in their true dispositions of heart and mind in executing the commands and teachings of Allah ﷻ.

One can analyze this example from another perspective. One can possibly say that Allah ﷻ gives these examples in the Qurān to differentiate the intrinsic attitudes of people. In other words, these examples can serve the purpose of a test or a trial to differentiate the different levels, the passing and the failing, the pure and the filthy, the humble and the arrogant.

The expression يُضِلُّ بِهِ كَثِيراً وَيَهْدِي بِهِ كَثِيراً وَمَا يُضِلُّ بِهِ إِلَّا الْفَاسِقِينَ [12] {البقرة/26} can indicate hidayah but one can ask the question of how can dalalah be possible with these examples and teachings as presented in the Qurān?

The Qurān is for the guidance, hidāyah of the person. Yet, with this general rule, one should always remember that a beneficial item can always be harmful for some exceptional people if often they misuse this general purpose of this item or if they have a wrong or improper intention of using this item.

---

11. The Messenger has believed in what was revealed to him from his Lord, and [so have] the believers. All of them have believed in Allah and His angels and His books and His messengers, [saying], "We make no distinction between any of His messengers." And they say, "We hear and we obey. [We seek] Your forgiveness, our Lord, and to You is the [final] destination."

12. Indeed, Allah is not timid to present an example—that of a mosquito or what is smaller than it. And those who have believed know that it is the truth from their Lord. But as for those who disbelieve, they say, "What did Allah intend by this as an example?" He misleads many thereby and guides many thereby. And He misleads not except the defiantly disobedient,

For a thirsty person may want to eat a cold watermelon. If there is knife, one can can cut this big watermelon and can benefit from the usage of this knife. Yet, if the same person uses the same knife to harm a person, then it is not used in its proper usage. Then, it becomes fisq, a misuse leading to chaos and self-destruction.

In this regard, the Qurān immediately explains this exceptional position of these people with إِلاَّ الْفَاسِقِينَ. The people who have the problem of fisq can actually destroy themselves if they have the wrong intention and attitude.

Especially, the word إِلاَّ underlines this contrary or exception of the general rule of the Qurān as the hidayah for everyone. Yet, if some people have the wrong intention and attitude, they can harm their ownselves.

May Allah ۞ protect us, Amïn.

[27]

الَّذِينَ يَنقُضُونَ عَهْدَ اللَّهِ مِن بَعْدِ مِيثَاقِهِ وَيَقْطَعُونَ مَا أَمَرَ اللَّهُ بِهِ أَن يُوصَلَ وَيُفْسِدُونَ فِي الأَرْضِ أُولَئِكَ هُمُ الْخَاسِرُونَ 13 {البقرة/27}

Innate Potential Powers of Humans

When we review the previous ayah, it ends as 14 يُضِلُّ بِهِ كَثِيراً وَيَهْدِي بِهِ كَثِيراً وَمَا يُضِلُّ بِهِ إِلاَّ الْفَاسِقِينَ {البقرة/26}. In this regard, this ayah details the people of fisq referred as fāsiq.

One can understand that Allah ۞ has created humans with potential power of three qualities. One is the potential power of intellect, reasoning, and critical thinking. This is called as brainpower referred as quwwa-I aqliyya.

The second is the potential power of temper, anger, indignation, resentment, and disgruntlement. This is called as power of temper as quwwa-I gadabiyya.

The third is the potential power of lust, desire and craving. This is called as power of desires as quwwa-I shawiyya.

---

13. Who break the covenant of Allah after contracting it and sever that which Allah has ordered to be joined and cause corruption on earth. It is those who are the losers.

14. Indeed, Allah is not timid to present an example—that of a mosquito or what is smaller than it. And those who have believed know that it is the truth from their Lord. But as for those who disbelieve, they say, "What did Allah intend by this as an example?" He misleads many thereby and guides many thereby. And He misleads not except the defiantly disobedient,

When these three powers in their potentiality is not balanced in action, then fisq, mischief can occur and display in personal, family, and social lives.

When these three potential powers are used in balance with guidance, then they can fulfill the needs of the person, family, and society and please Allah ﷻ.

The guidance is with the Qurān and Sunnah of Rasulullah ﷺ, as exempliefied by the pious salaf, precedors.

Breaking the Natural Divine Promise

When we review the ayah, there is an emphasis of breaking the promise of humans as mentioned with الَّذِينَ يَنقُضُونَ عَهْدَ اللَّهِ مِن بَعْدِ مِيثَاقِهِ.

In this regard, Allah ﷻ gave all humans these three potential powers and qualities. In the universe, and in our interactions with the universe, there are constant signs, ayahs from Allah ﷻ. In these engagements, humans with their free will is expected to implement their natural divine promise that they made with Allah ﷻ.

The natural can be also referred as fitri. In this regard, using these three powers of potentialities with balance are all in the range of fitri, natural engagements. In this regard, this is a promise of the person with Allah ﷻ that in their original creation that they were going to fulfill their enagements according to the requirements and natural disposition of their creation. One can call this as a qawlu bala in terminonlogy.

Yet, when the person engages him or herself with the extremes of these potential powers referred as ifrād and tafrìd in terminology, then the person breaks their natural stance of their promise as mentioned الَّذِينَ يَنقُضُونَ عَهْدَ اللَّهِ مِن بَعْدِ مِيثَاقِهِ.

The Divine teachings through the scriptures, the Qurān, and life of Rasulullah ﷺ teach and remind us how to be fitri, and natural befitting our enagements and choices according to our factory usage of creation. In this regard, one can view the Qurān as their factory manual as mentioned [15] لَقَدْ أَنزَلْنَا إِلَيْكُمْ كِتَابًا فِيهِ ذِكْرُكُمْ أَفَلَا تَعْقِلُونَ {الأنبياء/10}.

---

15. We have certainly sent down to you a Book in which is your mention. Then will you not reason?

Middle Way

When we analyze the teaching of middle way in Islam, one can realize that this concept also present in other religions such as Buddhism, Hinduism and very apparent in Sikkhism and others. One can deduce from here that Allah ☙ sent at different times different prophets, messengers and leads with the same critical, core and essential teachings. These common teachings are critical in the establishment and maintenance of personal, familial and social lives.

The notion of middle way can be defined as the understanding of nothing being extererme in the above mentioned three innate potential powers in an individual.

The extremities can then reflect on group levels of familial, kinship, social and even communal engagements.

The extremities or distancing oneself from middle-way can be an explicit and implicit rebelillion to the innate natural tendencies of all creation, universe and eco-system. These tendencies of extremisms cause the natural social structure and order to break into the ideas, and movements of unleashed extemeities of anger, lust and demagocy.

Unleashed anger in personal, familial and partner relationships can cause the popularized terms of all types of (mental, verbal and physical) abuse, oppression, and bullying in our modern terms.

Unleashed lust in relationships can cause the popularized terms of obesity, rape and assault.

Unleashed demagocy in politics, policy-making and governmental levels can cause wars, killing, position and power struggles.

One can see that although we have these innate potential powers of anger, lust, and intellect, they need guidance to stay on the middle-way.

Although all the law-enforcements in modern societies are designed to keep the people in middle way by force and fear, the enforemcents in religions entail teachings to instill the not an accountability in the world but an accountability by the One, Allah, God, Adonai as referred our to One and Only Creator. Karma concept in Buddhism and Hinduism can indicate the similar concepts of ensuring middle-way of these three innate potential powers of humans to be kept in middle-way and balance without abusing, oppressing and harming others and oneself.

One should remember that the extremities in the personal lives lead the extremities in group relations. In this regard, the extremes in familial and social lives cause the chaos and destruction in the world as mentioned وَيُفْسِدُونَ فِي الأَرْض. Fasād is translated as chaos, destruction and disunity due to these extremities.

Extremities in Brainpower & Imān

One of the extremities can occur in the potential power of intellect, reasoning, and critical thinking. This can be called as also extremities brainpower.

Extremities in brainpower can have an inverse relation with the imān and ittiqād, the belief of the person.

When the person does not know the limits of their intellect with the realities of adab especially in the encounters of Divine Transcedent Reality of Allah ﷻ, then he or she can go either in the valleys of magdubi alayhim or addālin as mentioned in Sûrah al-Fatiha as الْمَغْضُوب عَلَيهِمْ وَلاَ الضَّالِّينَ.

One extremity can occur in the encounter of adab with Allah ﷻ by not knowing the limits of adab and normalizing disrespectful attitude with Rabbul Alamìn leading to الْمَغْضُوب عَلَيهِمْ. In this regard, Shaytān is the prime example of this and his followers from the humans and jinn.

Another extremity can occur in the encounter with Allah ﷻ by not knowing the limits of adab of knowledge about Allah ﷻ. The adab of knowledge about the Infinite Transcedent Reality requires to know Allah ﷻ with the limits and boundaries of the Qurān and Sunnah for us and with the limits and boundaries of the prior scriptures such as Tawrah and teachings of Ibrahim as, Ishaq, Yaqub as, Musa as and other prophets and messengers the sunnah. Yet, people's absence of adab in this regard talking and estimating and mentally wandering without any adab is another extremity leading to الضَّالِّينَ. In this regard, Shaytān purposefully engages people to wander without any adab and proof from Allah ﷻ with their own so called "religious experience" and "inspirations."

Extremities in Temperament & Anger

The second is the potential power of temper, anger, indignation, resentment, and disgruntlement. This is called as power of temper as quwwa-I gadabiyya.

One should remember that Allah ﷻ has enabled different innate potential powers. Quwwai gadabiyya is another useful and healthy innate power if one knows how to tune it in the middle way.

When this innate power is in extremes, then chaos in family and social lives can be dominant.

Especially, when we talk about in interactions of a person with another person, one can call this as group, familial, friendship, professional or social interactions.

Our interactions with others can be analyzed in the fields of sociology and communication with the popular expression of "group" or "peer" dynamics.

In these engagements, the harm or destruction of chaos can be at multi-levels compared to the harms at personal level.

When a person has an extremity in oneself and when it is private, the effect of this harm can be limited somehow at the life of that individual.

Yet, when this individual's harm due to the extremities becomes public and start affecting others while this person is interacting with others, then the effects of this harm can be multiple and widespread like a fire spreading in a forest quickly.

Therefore, the studies of sociology and communication can be critical to focus on the parameters of these group related interactions, effects, leading to either structure and order or chaos and destruction. These group related interactions can be in a formal institution such as a government, country, constitution and in various steps of policy formation in organizations. These group related interactions can be in informal or formal institutions such as in a family between the parents and children, or between the spouses, or between the siblings. These group related interactions can be in informal settings between friends or peers.

Yet, before these interactions, one should be trained at an individual level of limits of these interactions. One can call these trainings as professionalism, or etiquettes. One can call this adab, respect and reverence in religious terms.

To enforce the prevention of these extremities, secular or non-secular institutions can form similar required trainings for their staff. They may name this such as "diversity training for prevention of gender and race discrimination," or "bullying trying program" or others.

In informal settings such as familial relations or so, one can call these trainings as "anger management" or "counseling" or others.

The goal of all these trainings are to prevent and minimize possible extremities in group interactions of a person.

The extremities that can be due to the vertical (top-down) authority holders affecting the subjects can be similar or different at peer or horizontal level interactions.

One can call the vertical or authority related interactions as abuse. There is an explicit extremity.

One can call horizontal or peer level interactions as peer pressure. This extremity may not be immediately visible for the person of a group due to the accepted harmful or extreme norms in a group. In this case, outsiders of this group try to make explicit or implicit trainings to inform the harms of these extremities so that one can realize these problems.

The explicit extremities can expect a hard power to solve a problem. For example, in a case of physical abuse, police enforcement can be necessary as a legal means of stopping this extremity. Although in this case, the individuals causing the extremity may not be educated, they can stop temporarily their abuse and extremity due to the fear of imprisonment.

The implicit extremities can require a softer power to solve the problem. For example, a child following another peer without any critical judgment of right or wrong can require constant and regular advice. Although the child may still continue the problem of finding herself in a harmful situation, yet constant training can build up a self-sufficient individual to prevent him or herself being in an extremity.

Yet, all these trainings, and educational critical thinking approaches are important in order to act in professional manner even though the person may not mean or agree to act in that manner.

In other words, if there is a smelly filth in a garbage, but if the garbage is closed tight, then the people may not be much bothered from its smell. But, if the garbage is open, then people will be much bothered from its smell.

Similarly, our raw-egos are filled with bad smell of spiritual diseases. Although our purpose of goal in life is to clean our hearts and mind from these mental and spiritual diseases, yet spiritual cleansing process is a life-long struggle until we die.

Yet, our humanly realities require interaction with others in familial, kinship, social and professional life. In these needed and necessary interactions, one should constrict and cover these evil covered spiritual diseases and follow the means and manners of adab, etiquette and professionalism. If not, if the cover of adab and professionalism is removed, then one can witness chaos, destruction and fitnah in family, kindship, social and even professional lives.

Today's liberty approaches do not consider the realities of these extremities. Many politicize and popularize these with sloganic liberty approaches. Yet, they don't practically realize innate powers of humans, and its proper way of modulation and balance for the middle way.

Extremities in Lust, Desire, & Craving

If one reviews the issues related with the extremities with lust, desire, and craving, one can realize another source of a problem leading to chaos and disorder.

The potential power of lust, desire and craving is referred as quwwa-I shawiyya.

In the extreme cases of this potential power, one can blindly follow their desires, and craving of their ego without consideration of their harms to others and themselves.

In gender relations, the person may want to only satisfy their desires without considering its harms, and potential destruction of personal lives. The offence of rapes as a physical abuse and violence and pregnancies due to the mental and emotional abuses of man are some of these examples of these extremities in gender relations.

Even in spousal relations, this extreme can so far that the person's only motivation in a relation can be only physical attraction and pleasure compared to the need of care, mercy, loyalty, and companionship in a relation.

Another extreme in this case can be related with the food. This extremity is today recognized as medical disease referred as obesity.

When we analyze the statement وَيُفْسِدُونَ فِي الأَرْضِ أُولَٰئِكَ هُمُ الْخَاسِرُونَ, there is a relationship between fisq and khusran.

Today, people of fisq can claim that they are in gain, achievement and success. Yet, the ayah mentions the opposite reality of today's understanding.

Fisq, chaos, and disorder can induce unhappiness and displeasure in this life. Its highest results with frustration is in the afterlife.

[255]

اللّهُ لاَ إِلَهَ إِلاَّ هُوَ الْحَيُّ الْقَيُّومُ لاَ تَأْخُذُهُ سِنَةٌ وَلاَ نَوْمٌ لَّهُ مَا فِي السَّمَاوَاتِ وَمَا فِي الأَرْضِ
مَن ذَا الَّذِي يَشْفَعُ عِنْدَهُ إِلاَّ بِإِذْنِهِ يَعْلَمُ مَا بَيْنَ أَيْدِيهِمْ وَمَا خَلْفَهُمْ وَلاَ يُحِيطُونَ بِشَيْءٍ مِّنْ
عِلْمِهِ إِلاَّ بِمَا شَاءَ وَسِعَ كُرْسِيُّهُ السَّمَاوَاتِ وَالأَرْضَ وَلاَ يَؤُودُهُ حِفْظُهُمَا وَهُوَ الْعَلِيُّ
الْعَظِيمُ ¹⁶ {البقرة/255}

True Knowledge, its Methodology and Knowledge about Allah ﷻ

When one analyzes the Ayatul-Kursi, besides many critical points of importance, one of the part is وَلاَ يُحِيطُونَ بِشَيْءٍ مِّنْ عِلْمِهِ إِلاَّ بِمَا شَاءَ.

One should remember that knowledge is an intellectual surrounding, encompassing, enclosing, encircling, bounding and bordering as especially emphasized with the word يُحِيطُونَ.

In this regard, it is required that the limited humans and creation cannot know Allah ﷻ truly, and fully. In this regard, the ayah can indicate this reality as ¹⁷ وَمَا قَدَرُوا اللّهَ حَقَّ قَدْرِهِ وَالأَرْضُ جَمِيعًا قَبْضَتُهُ يَوْمَ الْقِيَامَةِ وَالسَّمَاوَاتُ مَطْوِيَّاتٌ بِيَمِينِهِ سُبْحَانَهُ وَتَعَالَى عَمَّا يُشْرِكُونَ {الزمر/67}. Especially, the expression underlines this as وَمَا قَدَرُوا اللّهَ حَقَّ قَدْرِهِ.

On the other hand, the approximations of knowledge of humans about Allah ﷻ can be only with guidance with the Fadl and Rahmah and Grace of Allah ﷻ through the scriptures, the Qurān and teachings of the prophets, and the Prophet, Rasulullah ﷺ.

The cases of trinity among Christians and increasingly abstract trends about afterlife among Jews are the cases and examples of mind related deviations without any proof of confirmation and guidance in the authentic and original scriptures from Rabbul Alamìn. This is

---

16. Allah—there is no deity except Him, the Ever-Living, the Sustainer of [all] existence. Neither drowsiness overtakes Him nor sleep. To Him belongs whatever is in the heavens and whatever is on the earth. Who is it that can intercede with Him except by His permission? He knows what is [presently] before them and what will be after them, and they encompass not a thing of His knowledge except for what He wills. His Kursi extends over the heavens and the earth, and their preservation tires Him not. And He is the Most High, the Most Great.
17. They have not appraised Allah with true appraisal, while the earth entirely will be [within] His grip on the Day of Resurrection, and the heavens will be folded in His right hand. Exalted is He and high above what they associate with Him.

mentioned many times in the Qurān with different formats. One of them is the question forms asked with أَمْ لَهُمْ as: [18]

أَمْ لَهُمْ آلِهَةٌ تَمْنَعُهُم مِّن دُونِنَا لَا يَسْتَطِيعُونَ نَصْرَ أَنفُسِهِمْ وَلَا هُم مِّنَّا يُصْحَبُونَ {الأنبياء/43}

قُلْ أَرَأَيْتُم شُرَكَاءكُمُ الَّذِينَ تَدْعُونَ مِن دُونِ اللَّهِ أَرُونِي مَاذَا خَلَقُوا مِنَ الْأَرْضِ أَمْ لَهُمْ شِرْكٌ فِي السَّمَاوَاتِ أَمْ آتَيْنَاهُمْ كِتَابًا فَهُمْ عَلَى بَيِّنَةٍ مِّنْهُ بَلْ إِن يَعِدُ الظَّالِمُونَ بَعْضُهُم بَعْضًا إِلَّا غُرُورًا {فاطر/40}

أَمْ لَهُمْ شُرَكَاء شَرَعُوا لَهُم مِّنَ الدِّينِ مَا لَمْ يَأْذَن بِهِ اللَّهُ وَلَوْلَا كَلِمَةُ الْفَصْلِ لَقُضِيَ بَيْنَهُمْ [19] وَإِنَّ الظَّالِمِينَ لَهُمْ عَذَابٌ أَلِيمٌ {الشورى/21}

قُلْ أَرَأَيْتُم مَّا تَدْعُونَ مِن دُونِ اللَّهِ أَرُونِي مَاذَا خَلَقُوا مِنَ الْأَرْضِ أَمْ لَهُمْ شِرْكٌ فِي السَّمَاوَاتِ اِئْتُونِي بِكِتَابٍ مِّن قَبْلِ هَذَا أَوْ أَثَارَةٍ مِّنْ عِلْمٍ إِن كُنتُمْ صَادِقِينَ {الأحقاف/4}

أَمْ لَهُمْ إِلَهٌ غَيْرُ اللَّهِ سُبْحَانَ اللَّهِ عَمَّا يُشْرِكُونَ {الطور/43}

Moreover, if there is an explicit methodology of a knowledge or information claimed to be from Rabbul Alamìn, Allah ﷻ, then one should bring it forth and besides the Qurān, Injìl, and Tawrah. This is mentioned very clearly, plausibility, cogently, logically, and commonsensically as:

اِئْتُونِي بِكِتَابٍ مِّن قَبْلِ هَذَا أَوْ أَثَارَةٍ مِّنْ عِلْمٍ إِن كُنتُمْ صَادِقِينَ {الأحقاف/4}

---

18. Or do they have gods to defend them other than Us? They are unable [even] to help themselves, nor can they be protected from Us. Say, "Have you considered your 'partners' whom you invoke besides Allah? Show me what they have created from the earth, or have they partnership [with Him] in the heavens? Or have We given them a book so they are [standing] on evidence therefrom? [No], rather, the wrongdoers do not promise each other except delusion."

19. Or have they other deities who have ordained for them a religion to which Allah has not consented? But if not for the decisive word, it would have been concluded between them. And indeed, the wrongdoers will have a painful punishment. Say, [O Muhammad], "Have you considered that which you invoke besides Allah? Show me what they have created of the earth; or did they have partnership in [creation of] the heavens? Bring me a scripture [revealed] before this or a [remaining] trace of knowledge, if you should be truthful." Or have they a deity other than Allah? Exalted is Allah above whatever they associate with Him.

أَمْ آتَيْنَاهُمْ كِتَابًا فَهُمْ عَلَى بَيِّنَةٍ مِّنْهُ بَلْ إِن يَعِدُ الظَّالِمُونَ بَعْضُهُم بَعْضًا إِلَّا غُرُورًا [20]
{40/فاطر}

أَمِ اتَّخَذُوا مِن دُونِهِ آلِهَةً قُلْ هَاتُوا بُرْهَانَكُمْ هَذَا ذِكْرُ مَن مَّعِيَ وَذِكْرُ مَن قَبْلِي بَلْ أَكْثَرُهُمْ
لَا يَعْلَمُونَ الْحَقَّ فَهُم مُّعْرِضُونَ {الأنبياء/24}

أَمْ آتَيْنَاهُمْ كِتَابًا مِّن قَبْلِهِ فَهُم بِهِ مُسْتَمْسِكُونَ {الزخرف/21}

In other words, if I make a statement as:

Statement A: "I know Zayd is a person who is like this…and who
is not like this…."

This is a statement but we don't know whether it is true or not.

There can be two ways to confirm the objectivity, truth and reality
of the above statement.

One way, is to ask Zayd and report the claims about himself, and
check if he agrees or not. In this regard, we assume that Zayd is a truthful
person, then whatever he says that will be the dominant and final reality
about himself. This way of knowledge of something as a reality takes the
precedence of other approximations of knowledge learning about Zayd.

When we analyze the ayahs of the Quran, Allah SWT mentions
about the Divine Self as [21]

اللَّهُ لَا إِلَهَ إِلَّا هُوَ لَيَجْمَعَنَّكُمْ إِلَى يَوْمِ الْقِيَامَةِ لَا رَيْبَ فِيهِ وَمَنْ أَصْدَقُ مِنَ اللَّهِ حَدِيثًا {النساء/87}

وَالَّذِينَ آمَنُواْ وَعَمِلُواْ الصَّالِحَاتِ سَنُدْخِلُهُمْ جَنَّاتٍ تَجْرِي مِن تَحْتِهَا الأَنْهَارُ خَالِدِينَ فِيهَا أَبَدًا وَعْدَ
اللَّهِ حَقًّا وَمَنْ أَصْدَقُ مِنَ اللَّهِ قِيلاً {النساء/122}

---

20. Say, "Have you considered your 'partners' whom you invoke besides Allah? Show me what
they have created from the earth, or have they partnership [with Him] in the heavens? Or
have We given them a book so they are [standing] on evidence therefrom? [No], rather, the
wrongdoers do not promise each other except delusion." Or have they taken gods besides
Him? Say, [O Muhammad], "Produce your proof. This [Qurán] is the message for those with me
and the message of those before me." But most of them do not know the truth, so they are
turning away. Or have We given them a book before the Qurán to which they are adhering?
21. Allah—there is no deity except Him. He will surely assemble you for [account on] the
Day of Resurrection, about which there is no doubt. And who is more truthful than Allah in
statement. But the ones who believe and do righteous deeds—We will admit them to gardens
beneath which rivers flow, wherein they will abide forever. [It is] the promise of Allah, [which
is] truth, and who is more truthful than Allah in statement.

In this regard, the critical phrases are mentioned as وَمَنْ أَصْدَقُ مِنَ اللهِ {النساء/122} and وَمَنْ أَصْدَقُ مِنَ اللهِ قِيلاً {النساء/87} حَدِيثًا.

Allah SWT shows the Absolute Truthfulness of the Divine self to remind the creation. Moreover, Allah SWT emphasizes about the knowledge of the Divine Self with a ta'kid as in the as شَهِدَ اللهُ أَنَّهُ لاَ إِلَهَ إِلاَّ هُوَ. This is mentioned in [22]

شَهِدَ اللهُ أَنَّهُ لاَ إِلَهَ إِلاَّ هُوَ وَالْمَلاَئِكَةُ وَأُولُواْ الْعِلْمِ قَائِمَاً بِالْقِسْطِ لاَ إِلَهَ إِلاَّ هُوَ الْعَزِيزُ الْحَكِيمُ {آل عمران/18}

After above renderings, how or what can a person or people claim about the knowledge of Allah SWT if that is contradicting how Allah SWT explains about the Divine Self in the scriptures? The logic and intellect require that all the renderings about mind and intellect related approaches can be deviations from the reality if they are conflicting with the Quran and sunnah and if these approaches and marifatullah are not performed under the guidance of the Quran and sunnah.

The other is approach understanding the reality of something can be that if there are number of people who know Zayd well, and spend some time with Zayd. Then, if these number of people agree on statement A, then one can approach this as something credible. If the people have some type of disagreements on statement A, then it can become questionable. If the people have full disagreement on statement A, then statement A can become fullly not credible.

Similarly, one can see the approaches second method with one's knowledge abut Allah ﷻ. Ahlullah are the people who most know Allah SWT and spend time with Allah ﷻ in the maqām of ihsān. Here is an example of ahlullah as [23] فَإِنَّ اللهَ هُوَ مَوْلَاهُ وَجِبْرِيلُ وَصَالِحُ الْمُؤْمِنِينَ وَالْمَلاَئِكَةُ بَعْدَ ذَلِكَ ظَهِيرٌ {التحريم/4}

مَن كَانَ عَدُوًّا للهِ وَمَلآئِكَتِهِ وَرُسُلِهِ وَجِبْرِيلَ وَمِيكَالَ فَإِنَّ اللهَ عَدُوٌّ لِّلْكَافِرِينَ {البقرة/98}

---

22. Allah witnesses that there is no deity except Him, and [so do] the angels and those of knowledge—[that He is] maintaining [creation] in justice. There is no deity except Him, t
23. If you two [wives] repent to Allah, [it is best], for your hearts have deviated. But if you cooperate against him—then indeed Allah is his protector, and Gabriel and the righteous of the believers and the angels, moreover, are [his] assistants. Whoever is an enemy to Allah and His angels and His messengers and Gabriel and Michael—then indeed, Allah is an enemy to the disbelievers.

These ahlullah as mentioned in the above ayahs are the Jibril as, Mikail as, all prophets, and all angels, and righteous believers. Then, one can ask what is their claim or declaration about Allah SWT? Then, this immediately follows as [24]

شَهِدَ اللَّهُ أَنَّهُ لاَ إِلَهَ إِلاَّ هُوَ وَالْمَلاَئِكَةُ وَأُولُواْ الْعِلْمِ قَائِماً بِالْقِسْطِ لاَ إِلَهَ إِلاَّ هُوَ الْعَزِيزُ الْحَكِيمُ {آل عمران/18}

آمَنَ الرَّسُولُ بِمَا أُنزِلَ إِلَيْهِ مِن رَّبِّهِ وَالْمُؤْمِنُونَ كُلٌّ آمَنَ بِاللّهِ وَمَلاَئِكَتِهِ وَكُتُبِهِ وَرُسُلِهِ لاَ نُفَرِّقُ بَيْنَ أَحَدٍ مِّن رُّسُلِهِ وَقَالُواْ سَمِعْنَا وَأَطَعْنَا غُفْرَانَكَ رَبَّنَا وَإِلَيْكَ الْمَصِيرُ {البقرة/285}

Ahlullah witness with their intellect, belief, basirah, qalb, and experience with certainty about the marifatullah as Allah ﷻ mentions about the Divine Self in the Qurān.

So, there is no disagreement of the reports. Similar to the mentioned example for the case of Zayd. Both what Zayd says about himself and what Zayd's friends say about Zayd, are all in agreement. Then, this knowledge and information becomes absolute, real, and certain.

One can find a similar methodology in the authentication of the hadith. If there are multiple narrations confirming the statement of Rasulullah ﷺ from different sahabah, the close friends and companions of Rasulullah ﷺ, then this knowledge becomes credible.

If one analyzes the above report within the life of the Prophet ﷺ, if this statement befits to the teachings of the Qurān, other narrations of the hadith and his ﷺ overall character and approaches, then this knowledge about the hadith becomes certain, absolute, and real. This highest level of authentication in truthfulness, and reality can be called mutawatir in terminology.

In this sense, alhamdulillah, we have a such a blessing that the ummah of Rasulullah ﷺ had used and established these critical methodological approaches immediately starting from the time of Rasulullah ﷺ with the Fadl, Rahmah and Grace of Allah ﷻ.

---

24. Allah witnesses that there is no deity except Him, and [so do] the angels and those of knowledge—[that He is] maintaining [creation] in justice. There is no deity except Him, the Exalted in Might, the Wise. The Messenger has believed in what was revealed to him from his Lord, and [so have] the believers. All of them have believed in Allah and His angels and His books and His messengers, [saying], "We make no distinction between any of His messengers." And they say, "We hear and we obey. [We seek] Your forgiveness, our Lord, and to You is the [final] destination."

This can be again another manifestation of the Divine Assurance of the protection of the authenticity of the Qurān and relatedly the hadith in the human realms through the causes. Alhamadulillah lil Qurān, waliRasulina wa lil Islām adada khalqik wa Rida Nafsika wa Zinata Arshik!

[285]

آمَنَ الرَّسُولُ بِمَا أُنزِلَ إِلَيْهِ مِن رَّبِّهِ وَالْمُؤْمِنُونَ كُلٌّ آمَنَ بِاللّهِ وَمَلآئِكَتِهِ وَكُتُبِهِ وَرُسُلِهِ لاَ نُفَرِّقُ بَيْنَ أَحَدٍ مِّن رُّسُلِهِ وَقَالُواْ سَمِعْنَا وَأَطَعْنَا غُفْرَانَكَ رَبَّنَا وَإِلَيْكَ الْمَصِيرُ ²⁵ {البقرة/285}

Adab of Imān

When we analyze the above verse, the expression وَقَالُواْ سَمِعْنَا وَأَطَعْنَا teaches us the critical adab of imān.

Imān is an adab. The real guidance and hidayah comes and follows after this adab present.

In this sense, adab of imān is a pre-requisite for the real guidance and hidayah from Allah ﷻ.

In this regard, adab of imān indicates adab with Allah ﷻ and adab with all the shi'ar that Allah ﷻ orders us to have adab with.

These can include the adab with the Qurān, Rasulullah ﷺ, sahabah, tabi'un, taba-tabi'un and all other pious salaf of ahlulullah.

In a broader sense, adab with imān includes the adab with other books such as the Tawrah, Injil, and all others, adab with all the anbiyā such as Ibrahim as, Musa as, Isa as and all others, adab with all the malalika such as Jibril as, Mikail as, Azrail as, Israfil as and all others.

One should remember that the expression mentions وَقَالُواْ سَمِعْنَا وَأَطَعْنَا.

The word قَالُواْ can indicate an external and verbal attitude of saying even though the person may not understand fully the teachings. This is part of the adab of imān. Even though the person may not understand fully yet, adab with Allah ﷻ requires following the commands of Allah ﷻ as a Muslim who submits him or herself to Allah ﷻ.

---

25. The Messenger has believed in what was revealed to him from his Lord, and [so have] the believers. All of them have believed in Allah and His angels and His books and His messengers, [saying], "We make no distinction between any of His messengers." And they say, "We hear and we obey. [We seek] Your forgiveness, our Lord, and to You is the [final] destination."

The word سَمِعْنَا can also indicate an external attitude of only hearing although the other senses may not be much involved. Similarly, adab of imān requires to submit oneself about what they hear from the authentic sources such as the Prophet ﷺ and ahlulullah to follow and practice these teachings.

Sûrah 3 – Al- Āl 'Imrān

[2]

The Name of Allah ﷻ: Al-Qayyûm & the Desire of Humans for an Unending Life but not Death

اللَّهُ لَا إِلَهَ إِلاَّ هُوَ الْحَيُّ الْقَيُّومُ ٢٦ {آل عمران/2}

Increasing one's knowledge about Allah ﷻ referred as marifatullah through the Names and Attributes of Allah ﷻ is very critical. In this regard, it is important have some knowledge about these Divine Names and Attributes even though the amount of this knowledge may be less than a drop size in an Infinite Ocean.

The Name and Attribute of Allah ﷻ as الْقَيُّومُ is important especially for humans who can feel approaching steps of death in the limit life consciousness, awareness and wakefulness.

Our fears of unknowns from death make us think and consider the questions such as:

► Is there a way not to die? This can be possibly indicated in the ayah as ٢٧ وَلَتَجِدَنَّهُمْ أَحْرَصَ النَّاسِ عَلَى حَيَاةٍ وَمِنَ الَّذِينَ أَشْرَكُواْ يَوَدُّ أَحَدُهُمْ لَوْ يُعَمَّرُ أَلْفَ سَنَةٍ وَمَا هُوَ بِمُزَحْزِحِهِ مِنَ الْعَذَابِ أَن يُعَمَّرَ وَاللّهُ بَصِيرٌ بِمَا يَعْمَلُونَ {البقرة/96}

► Can we be infinite? This can be possibly indicated in the ayah as ٢٨ {الأنبياء/8} وَمَا جَعَلْنَاهُمْ جَسَدًا لَّا يَأْكُلُونَ الطَّعَامَ وَمَا كَانُوا خَالِدِينَ

---

26. Allah—there is no deity except Him, the Ever-Living, the Sustainer of existence.
27. And you will surely find them the most greedy of people for life—[even] more than those who associate others with Allah. One of them wishes that he could be granted life a thousand years, but it would not remove him in the least from the [coming] punishment that he should be granted life. And Allah is Seeing of what they do.
28. And We did not make the prophets forms not eating food, nor were they immortal [on earth].

► I know everyone dies but is there an exception for me at least? This can be possibly indicated in the ayah as [29] وَمَا جَعَلْنَا لِبَشَرٍ مِّن قَبْلِكَ الْخُلْدَ أَفَإِنْ مَّتَّ فَهُمُ الْخَالِدُونَ {الأنبياء/34} كُلُّ نَفْسٍ ذَائِقَةُ الْمَوْتِ وَنَبْلُوكُم بِالشَّرِّ وَالْخَيْرِ فِتْنَةً وَإِلَيْنَا تُرْجَعُونَ {الأنبياء/35}

If we try to approach these questions with the Name and Attribute of Allah الْقَيُّومُ ﷻ, one can possible relieve oneself with the approaching agony of death.

Allah ﷻ is الْقَيُّومُ. This Name and Attribute of Allah ﷻ that indicates and requires Ahadiyyah , Uniqueness, and Oneness of Allah ﷻ.

The notion of death, existence or non-existence are all valid for the beings who are created, and existent with the creation. For creation, there a starting point. For humans, with their awareness, consciousness and awareness, it is very painful to think and consider a possibility of "non-existence" after being existent.

One can feel the pain of this agony and fear in the expression of this possibility as [30] أَيَعِدُكُمْ أَنَّكُمْ إِذَا مِتُّمْ وَكُنتُمْ تُرَابًا وَعِظَامًا أَنَّكُم مُّخْرَجُونَ {المؤمنون/35} هَيْهَاتَ هَيْهَاتَ لِمَا تُوعَدُونَ {المؤمنون/36} إِنْ هِيَ إِلَّا حَيَاتُنَا الدُّنْيَا نَمُوتُ وَنَحْيَا وَمَا نَحْنُ بِمَبْعُوثِينَ {المؤمنون/37}.

When the people of kufr considers, thinks and verbalizes this possibility, one can clearly this frustration, agony, and pain in the phrase as هَيْهَاتَ هَيْهَاتَ.

One can realize the pain of this agony of the possibility of non-existence with full pessimism and darkness in the expression as أَيَعِدُكُمْ أَنَّكُمْ إِذَا مِتُّمْ وَكُنتُمْ تُرَابًا وَعِظَامًا أَنَّكُم مُّخْرَجُونَ {المؤمنون/35}. Especially, the expression إِذَا مِتُّمْ وَكُنتُمْ تُرَابًا وَعِظَامًا can vividly picturize their mental state of depression before they die. They put themselves in the dark valleys of pessimism and darkness due to their engagements of kufr. SubhanAllah! These people live but they are in pain in their lives.

May Allah ﷻ protect us from the dark points of kufr, Amīn.

Allah ﷻ is far and beyond from human constructions of creation as mentioned [31] أَللهُ الصَّمَدُ {الإخلاص/2}.

---

29. And We did not grant to any man before you eternity [on earth]; so if you die—would they be eternal? Every soul will taste death. And We test you with evil and with good as trial; and to Us you will be returned.

30. Does he promise you that when you have died and become dust and bones that you will be brought forth [once more]? How far, how far, is that which you are promised. Life is not but our worldly life—we die and live, but we will not be resurrected.

31. Allah, the Eternal Refuge.

The concepts of birth and giving birth are humanly realities of existence, death, and life. Allah ﷻ is far and beyond from human constructions as mentioned [32] {الإخلاص/3} لَمْ يَلِدْ وَلَمْ يُولَدْ.

In this regard, Allah ﷻ has the Absolute, Incessant, Continuous Life as can be indicated with الْحَيُّ. Yet, this life or existence is not like humans or creations. Allah ﷻ is الْقَيُّومُ. Allah ﷻ is. Everything and everyone depends on Allah ﷻ and Allah ﷻ is not dependent on anything as mentioned اللَّهُ الصَّمَدُ {الإخلاص/2} لَمْ يَلِدْ وَلَمْ يُولَدْ {الإخلاص/3}

In this sense, all the Names of Allah ﷻ such as Ahadiyyah, Qayyumiyah, Samadiyyah and all others require the Uniqueness and No Equivalency as mentioned [33] {الإخلاص/4} وَلَمْ يَكُن لَّهُ كُفُوًا أَحَدٌ.

Yet, if this the Absolute Reality, and it is, one can ask the reflections of continuity in life from Allah ﷻ as this is a desire for almost all humans. Allah ﷻ mentions as "ask for it, I will respond" as mentioned [34] وَقَالَ رَبُّكُمُ ادْعُونِي أَسْتَجِبْ لَكُمْ إِنَّ الَّذِينَ يَسْتَكْبِرُونَ عَنْ عِبَادَتِي سَيَدْخُلُونَ جَهَنَّمَ دَاخِرِينَ {غافر/60}.

One of the examples of this category is that Allah ﷻ bestows and reminds us the category of shuda that they don't have the agony of death. This is mentioned in [35] وَلَا تَحْسَبَنَّ الَّذِينَ قُتِلُواْ فِي سَبِيلِ اللَّه أَمْوَاتًا بَلْ أَحْيَاء عِندَ رَبِّهِمْ يُرْزَقُونَ {آل عمران/169}

Allahumma Ja'alna minhum fi waqtil al-Khayril al-hayātinā, Amìn.

In its general category, due to Rahmah, Fadl and Grace of Allah ﷻ that there is the akhirah, afterlife. If all creation, especially humans are in need and desire of this continuation of life after existence, then Allah ﷻ responds their need as the Rabb ﷻ to continue the life in akhirah.

In this regards, when one reviews and studies different Names and Attributes of Allah ﷻ, one can deduce this with certainty that there should be the afterlife as bestowed by Allah ﷻ especially due to the Names and Attributes of Allah ﷻ such as Ar-Rahman, As-Samiu', Al-Basìr, As-Salam, Zal-Jalali wal Ikrām, al-Karìm, al-Hannān, al-Mannān, al-Zāhir, al-Bātin and al-Mujìbu al-Daa'wāt, and Ar-Rahìm.

The Name and Attribute of Allah ﷻ as الْحَيُّ الْقَيُّومُ can imply the reflections of these Names and Attributes on humans and creation in the afterlife as continuation of their life, and existence with the Fadl

---

32. He neither begets nor is born,
33. Nor is there to Him any equivalent."
34. And your Lord says, "Call upon Me; I will respond to you." Indeed, those who disdain My worship will enter Hell [rendered] contemptible.
35. The truth is from your Lord, so do not be among the doubters.

وَالَّذِينَ آمَنُواْ وَعَمِلُواْ الصَّالِحَاتِ سَنُدْخِلُهُمْ ³⁶ as mentioned and Grace of Allah ﷻ
جَنَّاتٍ تَجْرِي مِن تَحْتِهَا الأَنْهَارُ خَالِدِينَ فِيهَا أَبَدًا لَهُمْ فِيهَا أَزْوَاجٌ مُطَهَّرَةٌ وَنُدْخِلُهُمْ ظِلاً ظَلِيلاً
{النساء/57}

أُوْلَئِكَ جَزَآؤُهُم مَّغْفِرَةٌ مِّن رَّبِّهِمْ وَجَنَّاتٌ تَجْرِي مِن تَحْتِهَا الأَنْهَارُ خَالِدِينَ فِيهَا وَنِعْمَ أَجْرُ
الْعَامِلِينَ {آل عمران/136}

Even the existence in Jahannam is a Rahmah compared to non-existence. When one reviews to expressions of خَالِدِينَ فِيهَا in the Qurān almost all comes with Jannah, there are few compared about Jahannam compared to Jannah. This itself show the Mercy, Rahmah, Fadl, Forgiveness, and Grace of Allah ﷻ is much more beyond the Adl, Justice of Allah ﷻ.

Knowing this with different Names and Attributes of Allah ﷻ as the marifatullah can relieve the person from the fears of death, non-existence, extinction, disappearance, loss, grief and terrorizing agonies.

SubhanAllah, Allah ﷻ is so Merciful on us and yet, we are so ungrateful.

May Allah ﷻ protect us from ungrateful attitudes of ours in our relationship with Allah ﷻ, Amìn.

May Allah ﷻ give us the appreciation for our Rabb, Allah ﷻ , Amìn.

May Allah ﷻ give us the adab to maintain adab in our relaitonships with Allah ﷻ and Rasulullah ﷺ, Amìn.

May Allah ﷻ treat us with Rahmah and Fadl, Mercy and Grace but not with Justice in this life and afterlife, Amìn.

---

36. But those who believe and do righteous deeds—We will admit them to gardens beneath which rivers flow, wherein they abide forever. For them therein are purified spouses, and We will admit them to deepening shade. Those—their reward is forgiveness from their Lord and gardens beneath which rivers flow [in Paradise], wherein they will abide eternally; and excellent is the reward of the [righteous] workers.

Juz 4

Sûrah 3 – Al- Āl 'Imrān

[96-97]

إِنَّ أَوَّلَ بَيْتٍ وُضِعَ لِلنَّاسِ لَلَّذِي بِبَكَّةَ مُبَارَكًا وَهُدًى لِّلْعَالَمِينَ {آل عمران/96} فِيهِ آيَاتٌ بَيِّنَاتٌ مَّقَامُ إِبْرَاهِيمَ وَمَن دَخَلَهُ كَانَ آمِنًا وَلِلَّهِ عَلَى النَّاسِ حِجُّ الْبَيْتِ مَنِ اسْتَطَاعَ إِلَيْهِ سَبِيلاً وَمَن كَفَرَ فَإِنَّ الله غَنِيٌّ عَنِ الْعَالَمِينَ ٣٧ {آل عمران/97}

Makkah is a Mubārak place. It is explicitly mentioned مُبَارَكًا. Makkah is a place of guidance. This is explicitly mentioned as بِبَكَّةَ مُبَارَكًا وَهُدًى. Makkah is a Mubarak place and a place of guidance for all with its inclusivity. This is mentioned with بِبَكَّةَ مُبَارَكًا وَهُدًى لِّلْعَالَمِينَ. In the tafāsir, it is mentioned that it is guidance for all because people of imān turn towards that direction when they are praying [1] [2].

With different usage of the word مُبَارَكًا, one can realize that a space or land can be Mubarak, blessed as mentioned بِبَكَّةَ مُبَارَكًا وَهُدًى لِّلْعَالَمِينَ. This is also mentioned in ٣٨ {المؤمنون/29} وَقُل رَّبِّ أَنزِلْنِي مُنزَلًا مُّبَارَكًا وَأَنتَ خَيْرُ الْمُنزِلِينَ and فَلَمَّا أَتَاهَا نُودِي مِن شَاطِئِ الْوَادِي الْأَيْمَنِ فِي الْبُقْعَةِ الْمُبَارَكَةِ مِنَ الشَّجَرَةِ أَن يَا مُوسَى إِنِّي أَنَا اللَّهُ رَبُّ الْعَالَمِينَ {القصص/30}.

An item such as a tree can be Mubarak as mentioned ٣٩ اللَّهُ نُورُ السَّمَاوَاتِ وَالْأَرْضِ مَثَلُ نُورِهِ كَمِشْكَاةٍ فِيهَا مِصْبَاحٌ الْمِصْبَاحُ فِي زُجَاجَةٍ الزُّجَاجَةُ كَأَنَّهَا كَوْكَبٌ دُرِّيٌّ يُوقَدُ مِن شَجَرَةٍ مُّبَارَكَةٍ زَيْتُونِةٍ لَّا شَرْقِيَّةٍ وَلَا غَرْبِيَّةٍ يَكَادُ زَيْتُهَا يُضِيءُ وَلَوْ لَمْ تَمْسَسْهُ نَارٌ نُّورٌ عَلَى نُورٍ يَهْدِي اللَّهُ لِنُورِهِ مَن يَشَاء وَيَضْرِبُ اللَّهُ الْأَمْثَالَ لِلنَّاسِ وَاللَّهُ بِكُلِّ شَيْءٍ عَلِيمٌ {النور/35}. This item can also be water as mentioned ٤٠ وَنَزَّلْنَا مِنَ السَّمَاء مَاء مُّبَارَكًا فَأَنبَتْنَا بِهِ جَنَّاتٍ وَحَبَّ الْحَصِيدِ {ق/9}

---

37. Indeed, the first House [of worship] established for mankind was that at Makkah—blessed and a guidance for the worlds. In it are clear signs [such as] the standing place of Abraham. And whoever enters it shall be safe. And [due] to Allah from the people is a pilgrimage to the House—for whoever is able to find thereto a way. But whoever disbelieves—then indeed, Allah is free from need of the worlds.

38. And say, 'My Lord, let me land at a blessed landing place, and You are the best to accommodate [us].'" But when he came to it, he was called from the right side of the valley in a blessed spot—from the tree, "O Moses, indeed I am Allah, Lord of the worlds."

39. Allah is the Light of the heavens and the earth. The example of His light is like a niche within which is a lamp, the lamp is within glass, the glass as if it were a pearly [white] star lit from [the oil of] a blessed olive tree, neither of the east nor of the west, whose oil would almost glow even if untouched by fire. Light upon light. Allah guides to His light whom He wills. And Allah presents examples for the people, and Allah is Knowing of all things.

40. And We have sent down blessed rain from the sky and made grow thereby gardens and grain from the harvest

A word, a phrase or a statement can be Mubarak as mentioned [41]

لَيْسَ عَلَى الْأَعْمَى حَرَجٌ وَلَا عَلَى الْأَعْرَجِ حَرَجٌ وَلَا عَلَى الْمَرِيضِ حَرَجٌ وَلَا عَلَى أَنفُسِكُمْ أَن تَأْكُلُوا مِن بُيُوتِكُمْ أَوْ بُيُوتِ آبَائِكُمْ أَوْ بُيُوتِ أُمَّهَاتِكُمْ أَوْ بُيُوتِ إِخْوَانِكُمْ أَوْ بُيُوتِ أَخَوَاتِكُمْ أَوْ بُيُوتِ أَعْمَامِكُمْ أَوْ بُيُوتِ عَمَّاتِكُمْ أَوْ بُيُوتِ أَخْوَالِكُمْ أَوْ بُيُوتِ خَالَاتِكُمْ أَوْ مَا مَلَكْتُم مَّفَاتِحَهُ أَوْ صَدِيقِكُمْ لَيْسَ عَلَيْكُمْ جُنَاحٌ أَن تَأْكُلُوا جَمِيعًا أَوْ أَشْتَاتًا فَإِذَا دَخَلْتُم بُيُوتًا فَسَلِّمُوا عَلَى أَنفُسِكُمْ تَحِيَّةً مِّنْ عِندِ اللَّهِ مُبَارَكَةً طَيِّبَةً كَذَلِكَ يُبَيِّنُ اللَّهُ لَكُمُ الْآيَاتِ لَعَلَّكُمْ تَعْقِلُونَ [42] {النور/61}

The teachings in the form of a book can be Mubarak such as the Qurān as mentioned [43] كِتَابٌ أَنزَلْنَاهُ إِلَيْكَ مُبَارَكٌ لِّيَدَّبَّرُوا آيَاتِهِ وَلِيَتَذَكَّرَ أُولُوا الْأَلْبَابِ {ص/92}

وَهَذَا كِتَابٌ أَنزَلْنَاهُ مُبَارَكٌ مُّصَدِّقُ الَّذِي بَيْنَ يَدَيْهِ وَلِتُنذِرَ أُمَّ الْقُرَى وَمَنْ حَوْلَهَا وَالَّذِينَ يُؤْمِنُونَ بِالْآخِرَةِ يُؤْمِنُونَ بِهِ وَهُمْ عَلَى صَلَاتِهِمْ يُحَافِظُونَ [44] {الأنعام/29}

وَهَذَا كِتَابٌ أَنزَلْنَاهُ مُبَارَكٌ فَاتَّبِعُوهُ وَاتَّقُواْ لَعَلَّكُمْ تُرْحَمُونَ {الأنعام/155}

The time can be Mubarak as the sacred time as mentioned [45] إِنَّا أَنزَلْنَاهُ فِي لَيْلَةٍ مُبَارَكَةٍ إِنَّا كُنَّا مُنذِرِينَ {الدخان/3}

One can review the terms such as sacred space, sacred time or sacred water within the descriptions of the Qurān.

---

41. There is not upon the blind [any] constraint nor upon the lame constraint nor upon the ill constraint nor upon yourselves when you eat from your [own] houses or the houses of your fathers or the houses of your mothers or the houses of your brothers or the houses of your sisters or the houses of your father's brothers or the houses of your father's sisters or the houses of your mother's brothers or the houses of your mother's sisters or [from houses] whose keys you possess or [from the house] of your friend. There is no blame upon you whether you eat together or separately. But when you enter houses, give greetings of peace upon each other—a greeting from Allah, blessed and good. Thus does Allah make clear to you the verses [of ordinance] that you may understand.

42. There is not upon the blind [any] constraint nor upon the lame constraint nor upon the ill constraint nor upon yourselves when you eat from your [own] houses or the houses of your fathers or the houses of your mothers or the houses of your brothers or the houses of your sisters or the houses of your father's brothers or the houses of your father's sisters or the houses of your mother's brothers or the houses of your mother's sisters or [from houses] whose keys you possess or [from the house] of your friend. There is no blame upon you whether you eat together or separately. But when you enter houses, give greetings of peace upon each other—a greeting from Allah, blessed and good. Thus does Allah make clear to you the verses [of ordinance] that you may understand.

43. [This is] a blessed Book which We have revealed to you, [O Muhammad], that they might reflect upon its verses and that those of understanding would be reminded.

44. And this is a Book which We have sent down, blessed and confirming what was before it, that you may warn the Mother of Cities and those around it. Those who believe in the Hereafter believe in it, and they are maintaining their prayers. And this [Qurán] is a Book We have revealed [which is] blessed, so follow it and fear Allah that you may receive mercy.

45. Indeed, We sent it down during a blessed night. Indeed, We were to warn [mankind].

Yet, we understand the land Makkah as a blessed place, Mubarak. One can consider today and in the history the incidents happened in Makkah around the Kabah referred as Haram.

There were times in the past where this blessed place either used opposite to its essential purpose when people used to worship idols. After Islām, there were times where there were some diseases or natural disasters that people were not able to visit or worship around it.

In these times, one can ask is this a deprivation from Allah ﷻ that we as Muslims don't deserve to visit Kabah and therefore, there are means or reasons preventing us? Or, even if one visits Kabah, when they encounter constructions, buildings, and extravagations that can easily flabbergast the person about these changes happening around Kabah in Makkah today.

Then, again one can ask to themselves, what is happening? What is the meaning of all these in the universal teachings of the Qurān and Sunnah of Rasulullah ﷺ? It is interesting to note that when Rasulullah ﷺ was forced to migrate, make hijrah, from Makkah to madina he ﷺ had a famous statement on the outskirts of Makkah with sadness that he ﷺ still loved Makkah but he was forced to leave [6] (Hadith #: 3925). This can show that even there is an evil happening in a blessed land, one should not blame the land due to the mischief of humans on that land. The land is still blessed and Mubarak. It is blessedness continues because it is assigned by Allah ﷻ. Yet, sometimes to be safe from the fitnah of people, one can or should leave a blessed land as the sunnah of Rasulullah ﷺ as he ﷺ himself did it [7].

In these perspectives, Makkah, Madinah, or sacred lands can be left in order to follow the sunnah of Rasulullah ﷺ if there is a mischief, fitnah or chaos displaying on these blessed lands.

One should remember that the source of chaos, fitnah or mischief is not the land but people or humans. Humans use the lands or even the sea to use them as a vehicle to demonstrate chaos or fithnah as mentioned [46] ظَهَرَ الْفَسَادُ فِي الْبَرِّ وَالْبَحْرِ بِمَا كَسَبَتْ أَيْدِي النَّاسِ لِيُذِيقَهُم بَعْضَ الَّذِي عَمِلُوا لَعَلَّهُمْ يَرْجِعُونَ {الروم/41}.

Therefore, the main purpose of hijrah or migration in Islām is to leave the people of fitnah or chaos wherever they are. Even if they are on

---

46. Corruption has appeared throughout the land and sea by [reason of] what the hands of people have earned so He may let them taste part of [the consequence of] what they have done that perhaps they will return [to righteousness].

the blessed lands, one does not stay on that land due to the blessedness of this land but leave that place primarily to ensure that they are safe from the people's fitnahs, destruction and chaos. If there is no safety and security, then one can not practice their own religion peacefully. The essence of life and existence requires peace.

[99]

أَفَأَمِنُواْ مَكْرَ اللَّهِ فَلاَ يَأْمَنُ مَكْرَ اللَّهِ إِلاَّ الْقَوْمُ الْخَاسِرُونَ ⁴⁷ {الأعراف/99}

Disease of Spiritual Safety

One should not be in the disposition of spiritual safety. Spiritual safety in this world leads to arrogance, unappreciation, ungratefulness. The case of Shaytān with angels and in his relationship with Allah ﷻ is due to this spiritual disease. Sometimes, the relative longevity can lead to spiritual safety in the form of hardening of the hearts as mentioned ⁴⁸ وَلَا يَكُونُوا كَالَّذِينَ أُوتُوا الْكِتَابَ مِن قَبْلُ فَطَالَ عَلَيْهِمُ الْأَمَدُ فَقَسَتْ قُلُوبُهُمْ وَكَثِيرٌ مِّنْهُمْ فَاسِقُونَ {الحديد/16}

A person can be in the apparent forms of fath, victories, and openings from Allah ﷻ. Yet, these critical dispositions necessitate the embodiment of gratitude to Allah ﷻ and istigfar in case if there is any self-claims of arrogance as shirk as mentioned ⁴⁹ إِذَا جَاء نَصْرُ أللَّهِ وَالْفَتْحُ {النصر/1} وَرَأَيْتَ النَّاسَ يَدْخُلُونَ فِي دِينِ اللَّهِ أَفْوَاجًا {النصر/2} فَسَبِّحْ بِحَمْدِ رَبِّكَ وَاسْتَغْفِرْهُ إِنَّهُ كَانَ تَوَّابًا {النصر/3}

At any time, these good seeming things can turn into a chaos to show the reality of the person as mentioned here as ⁵⁰ أَفَأَمِنُواْ مَكْرَ أللَّهِ فَلَا يَأْمَنُ مَكْرَ اللَّهِ إِلاَّ الْقَوْمُ الْخَاسِرُونَ {الأعراف/99}.

In these forms of ibtila, test or istidraj a good-seeming evil, one can be in the groups of magdubi alayhim and/or wa ladallin.

---

47. Then did they feel secure from the plan of Allah? But no one feels secure from the plan of Allah except the losing people.

48. Has the time not come for those who have believed that their hearts should become humbly submissive at the remembrance of Allah and what has come down of the truth? And let them not be like those who were given the Scripture before, and a long period passed over them, so their hearts hardened; and many of them are defiantly disobedient.

49. hen the victory of Allah has come and the conquest, And you see the people entering into the religion of Allah in multitudes, Then exalt [Him] with praise of your Lord and ask forgiveness of Him. Indeed, He is ever Accepting of repentance.

50. Then did they feel secure from the plan of Allah? But no one feels secure from the plan of Allah except the losing people.

When one considers the critical repetition of the ayah in each prayer at least thirteen times a day as [51] صِرَاطَ الَّذِينَ أَنْعَمتَ عَلَيهِمْ غَيرِ المَغضُوبِ عَلَيهِمْ وَلَا الضَّالِّينَ {الفاتحة/7} is a form of taking refuge to Allah ﷻ. The repetition of this ayah in each prayer at least thirteen times a day is taking refuge from the outcome of أَفَأَمِنُوا مَكْرَ اللَّهِ فَلاَ يَأْمَنُ مَكْرَ اللَّهِ إِلاَّ الْقَوْمُ الْخَاسِرُونَ {الأعراف/99}.

In this regard, people who are in the traps of spiritual safety as indicated in أَفَأَمِنُوا مَكْرَ اللَّهِ فَلاَ يَأْمَنُ مَكْرَ اللَّهِ إِلاَّ الْقَوْمُ الْخَاسِرُونَ {الأعراف/99} lead to the next step of المَغضُوبِ عَلَيهِمْ and الضَّالِّينَ {الفاتحة/7}.

May Allah ﷻ protect us from spiritual safety, Amìn.

May Allah ﷻ protect us to be among the ones of المَغضُوبِ عَلَيهِمْ and الضَّالِّينَ, Amìn.

May Allah ﷻ give us the embodiment of tasbìh and istigfar, Dhikrullah to be among the ones of فَسَبِّحْ بِحَمْدِ رَبِّكَ وَاسْتَغْفِرْهُ, Amìn.

[159]

[52] فَبِمَا رَحْمَةٍ مِّنَ اللَّهِ لِنتَ لَهُمْ وَلَوْ كُنتَ فَظًّا غَلِيظَ الْقَلْبِ لَانفَضُّوا مِنْ حَوْلِكَ فَاعْفُ عَنْهُمْ وَاسْتَغْفِرْ لَهُمْ وَشَاوِرْهُمْ فِي الْأَمْرِ فَإِذَا عَزَمْتَ فَتَوَكَّلْ عَلَى اللَّهِ إِنَّ اللَّهَ يُحِبُّ الْمُتَوَكِّلِينَ {آل عمران/159}

The Real Achievement

One can ask Allah ﷻ to give openings on the path of Allah ﷻ through dawah, tabligh and people's engagement with the Qurān, Rasulullah ﷺ and Islām.

One can ask these true openings for Muslims and non-Muslims from Allah ﷻ. One should ask that that Allah ﷻ is pleased with all these openings, futuhāt but these are not istridrāj that they are poisonous honey on the path of Allah ﷻ.

Yet, one should remember that all the true openings on the path of Allah ﷻ that Allah ﷻ is pleased, are still given by Allah ﷻ. Therefore, one can and should ask the 'I'ana of Allah ﷻ for these real and true openings as mentioned [53] نَعْبُدُ وَإِيَّاكَ نَسْتَعِينُ {الفاتحة/5}. It is again from the

---

51. The path of those upon whom You have bestowed favor, not of those who have evoked [Your] anger or of those who are astray.
52. So by mercy from Allah, [O Muhammad], you were le fcnient with them. And if you had been rude [in speech] and harsh in heart, they would have disbanded from about you. So pardon them and ask forgiveness for them and consult them in the matter. And when you have decided, then rely upon Allah. Indeed, Allah loves those who rely [upon Him].
53. It is You we worship and You we ask for help.

Fadl and Rahmah of Allah ﷻ that Allah ﷻ is teaching us to ask help from Allah ﷻ in Sûrah Fatiha everyday and constantly, initially, and regularly, SubhanAllah!

One of the conditions of these openings is establishing a prophetic atmosphere of Layyinah as mentioned with لِنتَ لَهُمْ. Yes, this critical atmosphere of Rasulullah ﷺ is the key revival of Allah ﷻ's message among Muslims and non-Muslims.

May Allah ﷻ give us this character of Layyin in following the path of Rasulullah ﷺ to please Allah ﷻ with billions of true and real openings, futuhāt, on the path of Allah ﷻ in our engagements with Muslims and non-Muslims, Amìn!

Layyin: The Prophetic Athmospere

One ask what does layyin mean? What is meant with لِنتَ لَهُمْ ?

Layyin is the Muhammadi ﷺ atmosphere of

- ► acceptance,
- ► tolerance,
- ► overseeing the faults,
- ► non-judgmental character,
- ► smiling,
- ► making ease and desiring easiness for people,
- ► comforting and solacing character,
- ► accepting everyone at their level with their gender, culture and ethnic background
- ► when people make mistake, asking forgiving them and asking forgiveness from Allah ﷻ for them.

The above list can go further as Rasulullah ﷺ never-ending guidance for all creation. Yet, one should really understand some of the appealing characters of the Prophet ﷺ is expressed and condensed with one word as layyin.

Yet, this enablement of being layyin is given and bestowed on Rasulullah ﷺ by Allah ﷻ as emphasized and underlined with فَبِمَا رَحْمَةٍ مِّنَ اللَّهِ لِنتَ لَهُمْ. In this sense, one can compare this similar perspective with

the repetition of the word بِإِذْنِي for Isa as in [54] وَإِذْ تَخْلُقُ مِنَ الطِّينِ كَهَيْئَةِ الطَّيْرِ
بِإِذْنِي فَتَنفُخُ فِيهَا فَتَكُونُ طَيْرًا بِإِذْنِي وَتُبْرِىءُ الأَكْمَهَ وَالأَبْرَصَ بِإِذْنِي وَإِذْ تُخْرِجُ الْمَوْتَى بِإِذْنِي
وَإِذْ كَفَفْتُ بَنِي إِسْرَائِيلَ عَنكَ إِذْ جِئْتَهُم بِالْبَيِّنَاتِ فَقَالَ الَّذِينَ كَفَرُواْ مِنْهُمْ إِنْ هَذَا إِلاَّ سِحْرٌ مُّبِينٌ
{المائدة/110}.

The Muhammadi ﷺ atmosphere of layyinah can be a miracle. This miracle as the embodied character of Rasulullah ﷺ can be similar to the miracles given to other prophets such as Isa as in the above ayah. Yet, all the miracles can set guidelines and the goal for humans to achieve similar to prophets in order to please Allah ﷻ.

In this perspective, one should constantly ask this Muhammadi ﷺ atmosphere and character of layyinah from Allah ﷻ for achievements and openings, futuhāt, in order to please Allah ﷻ.

Peak of Layyinah

When we consider above characters of Rasulullah ﷺ expressed with layyinah, one should remember one of the utmost and peak parts of being layyin is when people make mistake, the person still forgives them and moreover asks forgiveness from Allah ﷻ for them.

Let's be honest and ask ourselves that who can do this?

When we get angry we lose ourselves, then we start destroying ourselves and others.

When we get angry if we try to control ourselves, we build up in ourselves this self-dialogue of hate, anger and dislike towards people who made us angry.

When we get angry in this state, how many of us can relieve ourselves from this anger and can move on as mentioned with the expression فَاعْفُ عَنْهُمْ ?

How many of us can move on and on top of it, ask Allah ﷻ to forgive them?

This is Rasulullah ﷺ. This is the essence and core of being layyin.

---

54. [The Day] when Allah will say, "O Jesus, Son of Mary, remember My favor upon you and upon your mother when I supported you with the Pure Spirit and you spoke to the people in the cradle and in maturity; and [remember] when I taught you writing and wisdom and the Torah and the Gospel; and when you designed from clay [what was] like the form of a bird with My permission, then you breathed into it, and it became a bird with My permission; and you healed the blind and the leper with My permission; and when you brought forth the dead with My permission; and when I restrained the Children of Israel from [killing] you when you came to them with clear proofs and those who disbelieved among them said, "This is not but obvious magic."

May Allah ﷻ make us and give the character of true layyinah of Rasulullah ﷺ to please Allah ﷻ, Amìn!

Counseling with People

One should remember the critical position of counseling and meeting with people for their inclusivity and embodiment of the teachings, and actions when they are listened and involved in decision-making. One can call this counseling with people as mashwarah or istiasarah as mentioned in شَاوِرْهُمْ فِي الأَمْرِ فَإِذَا عَزَمْتَ فَتَوَكَّلْ عَلَى اللهِ.

In this regard, ordering people and accepting them to follow is not a prophetic character. Many times, Rasulullah ﷺ changed his decision and followed the decision of others in the results of mashwarah or istisharah [8].

Yet, one should constantly, initially and regularly maintain the required counseling with Allah ﷻ even when the person is in the counseling with others. Sometimes or often, people will have differences of opinions that may not be the best fit and can cause disturbance and chaos as conflicts and disagreements.

Although it is from sunnatullah to implement the mechanism of mashwarah, counseling with people as also referred as democracy today, one should always but always remember that the real guidance with collective mind of decision making is still with the enablement of Allah ﷻ.

وَإِن يُرِيدُواْ أَن يَخْدَعُوكَ فَإِنَّ حَسْبَكَ أُلله هُوَ الَّذِيَ أَيَّدَكَ This is mentioned as [55] بِنَصْرِهِ وَبِالْمُؤْمِنِينَ {الأنفال/62} وَأَلَّفَ بَيْنَ قُلُوبِهِمْ لَوْ أَنفَقْتَ مَا فِي الأَرْضِ جَمِيعاً مَّا أَلَّفَتْ بَيْنَ قُلُوبِهِمْ وَلَكِنَّ اللهَ أَلَّفَ بَيْنَهُمْ إِنَّهُ عَزِيزٌ حَكِيمٌ {الأنفال/63}

Therefore, mashwarah or collective mind of decision making through counseling is only another means or reasons that Allah ﷻ created to be followed as today's scientific approach of social disciplines. Yet, we don't replace the means with the real. Allah ﷻ is the Real Doer beyond and above all the Reasons.

---

55. But if they intend to deceive you—then sufficient for you is Allah. It is He who supported you with His help and with the believers And brought together their hearts. If you had spent all that is in the earth, you could not have brought their hearts together; but Allah brought them together. Indeed, He is Exalted in Might and Wise.

Counseling with Allah ﷻ

The detailed methods of psychology, counseling or psycho-therapy are all useless and not much fruitful on working behavioral changes if the person does not recognize that one should first do constant and initial and regular counseling with Rabbul Alamìn. Other types of humanly counseling can come accordingly as the reflection of the first initial required constant and regular counseling.

One can remember Sûrah Mujadala emphasing this approach for a woman, sahabiyah who initially, constantly and regularly go to Allah ﷻ for counseling as mentioned with the expression وَتَشْتَكِي إِلَى اللهِ in 56 قَدْ سَمِعَ اللَّهُ قَوْلَ الَّتِي تُجَادِلُكَ فِي زَوْجِهَا وَتَشْتَكِي إِلَى اللهِ وَاللَّهُ يَسْمَعُ تَحَاوُرَكُمَا إِنَّ اللَّهَ سَمِيعٌ بَصِيرٌ {المجادلة/1}

Then, this sahabiyah goes to the most expert and qualified counselor on the history of earth as a human who is Rasulullah ﷺ after the initial counseling with Allah ﷻ [1].

It is also sometimes rationalize the position of Yaqûb as with his children. One can ask how he as endured all these difficulties with his children and still maintained the position of layyinah at another level? The answer is very straightforward. Yaqub as did only but only counseling with Allah ﷻ as mentioned 57 قَالَ إِنَّمَا أَشْكُو بَثِّي وَحُزْنِي إِلَى آللِه وَأَعْلَمُ مِنَ اللَّهِ مَا لاَ تَعْلَمُونَ {يوسف/86}.

One should remember that our purpose of creation and existence entails and requires to go to Allah ﷻ for our needs as mentioned in Sûrah Fatiha constantly as 58 وَإِيَّاكَ نَسْتَعِينُ {الفاتحة/5}.

A person who takes others as their helpers initially, constantly and regularly other than Allah ﷻ will be always but always in frustration and loss. This attitude actually can be referred as shirk or kufr in its technical term.

After this attitude of imãn requiring the person having initial, constant and regular asking help from Allah ﷻ, then others can be called all means or reasons that Allah ﷻ can enable them. Yet, in this regard

---

56. Certainly has Allah heard the speech of the one who argues with you, [O Muhammad], concerning her husband and directs her complaint to Allah. And Allah hears your dialogue; indeed, Allah is Hearing and Seeing.
57. He said, "I only complain of my suffering and my grief to Allah, and I know from Allah that which you do not know.
58. It is You we worship and You we ask for help.

one should follow the proper means and reasons with always expecting the results and change from Allah ﷻ.

Yet, there are some ahlullah who even does not want to shadow their relationship with Allah ﷻ through the weak means. Therefore, even when they have problems they keep it between them and Allah ﷻ and only asking help only from Allah ﷻ but not from others similar to the case of Yaqub as mentioned above.

One can also view this approach in the case of Ibrahim as when he was thrown in the fire. He as did not want even the means of angels helping him [1].Another example of this can be Zakariyya as in his need for a child. When he observed Maryam as, he fully realized this and asked his need from Allah ﷻ in his prayer. Then, the means and reasons were all nullified and invalidated as both Zakariyya as and his wife were very old but yet, they had a pious child, Yahya as [1].

Assurance from Allah ﷻ

SubhanAllah! This is very important in true Muslim counseling.

Allah ﷻ is the True Listener, Helper and Solver of all problems. In this sense, one can think I am telling my problems to Allah ﷻ, but is there a response? Is Allah ﷻ listening me? Or, "Am I talking to myself, astagfirullah?" These are all possible nafs related renderings especially with the temptations of Shaytān.

Yet, Allah ﷻ assures us in a similar problem as mentioned in Sûrah Mujadalah that Allah ﷻ is As-Sami' and Allah ﷻ is listening. This is mentioned in the ayah [59] قَدْ سَمِعَ ٱللَّهُ قَوْلَ ٱلَّتِي تُجَادِلُكَ فِي زَوْجِهَا وَتَشْتَكِي إِلَى ٱللَّهِ وَٱللَّهُ يَسْمَعُ تَحَاوُرَكُمَا إِنَّ ٱللَّهَ سَمِيعٌ بَصِيرٌ {المجادلة/1}. This assurance is repeated in this ayah three times that Allah ﷻ is Listening and Hearing with ta'kid, emphasis as قَدْ سَمِعَ ٱللَّهُ, and with another takid as وَٱللَّهُ يَسْمَعُ تَحَاوُرَكُمَا and with the final and underlining ta'kid as إِنَّ ٱللَّهَ سَمِيعٌ بَصِيرٌ, SubhanAllah!

Even, one can remember this assurance of Allah ﷻ in every salah when stand up from ruku', we say "Sami'a Allahu Li man Hamidah" that "Allah ﷻ hears and listens the ones who are in constant embodiment of Hamd and Shukr to Allah ﷻ" Hamd and Shukr to Allah ﷻ is the essence of imān. Kufr is the absence of the hamd and shukr to Allah ﷻ.

---

59. Certainly has Allah heard the speech of the one who argues with you, [O Muhammad], concerning her husband and directs her complaint to Allah. And Allah hears your dialogue; indeed, Allah is Hearing and Seeing.

Therefore, in each salah, the special connection of the person with imãn is constantly being assured with the expression "Sami'a Allahu Li man Hamidah" that "Allah 🕮 hears and listens the ones who are in constant embodiment of Hamd and Shukr to Allah 🕮" so that the person does not hesitate with delusional attacks of Shaytãn and his or her own nafs. Astagfirullah!

[192-194] [60]

رَبَّنَا إِنَّكَ مَن تُدْخِلِ النَّارَ فَقَدْ أَخْزَيْتَهُ وَمَا لِلظَّالِمِينَ مِنْ أَنصَارٍ {آل عمران/192} رَبَّنَا إِنَّنَا سَمِعْنَا مُنَادِيًا يُنَادِي لِلإِيمَانِ أَنْ آمِنُواْ بِرَبِّكُمْ فَآمَنَّا رَبَّنَا فَاغْفِرْ لَنَا ذُنُوبَنَا وَكَفِّرْ عَنَّا سَيِّئَاتِنَا وَتَوَفَّنَا مَعَ الأبْرَارِ {آل عمران/193} رَبَّنَا وَآتِنَا مَا وَعَدتَّنَا عَلَى رُسُلِكَ وَلاَ تُخْزِنَا يَوْمَ الْقِيَامَةِ إِنَّكَ لاَ تُخْلِفُ الْمِيعَادَ {آل عمران/194}

The Real Embarrassment

Embarrassment or hayã can be a state of the heart and mind that today, we increasingly loose in the current popular culture especially with globalization via internet and media.

Hayã as modesty is becoming increasingly a lost term. Hayã with people, hayã with creation and most importantly hayã with Allah 🕮 are all becoming theoretical concepts. Ultimately, hayã with Allah 🕮 leads to adab with Allah 🕮 and accordingly adab with teachers, elders, parents and others.

A person of hayã imbedded in this culture can easily lose this valuable trait due to being considered as an outcast in this society. Especially, when teachings of hayã are frowned upon and actually, having no hayã or adab is constantly presented and encouraged at all levels of education as part of the critical thinking and liberal approaches and freedom.

In these societies and times of absence of hayã and adab, what should one do not to be hopeless or pessimistic?

---

60. Our Lord, indeed whoever You admit to the Fire—You have disgraced him, and for the wrongdoers there are no helpers. Our Lord, indeed we have heard a caller calling to faith, [saying], 'Believe in your Lord,' and we have believed. Our Lord, so forgive us our sins and remove from us our misdeeds and cause us to die with the righteous. Our Lord, and grant us what You promised us through Your messengers and do not disgrace us on the Day of Resurrection. Indeed, You do not fail in [Your] promise."

The Quranic ayah above especially underlines the concept of real embarrassment with the word أَخْزَيْتَهُ.

Hayā requires minimizing the embarrassments. The real embarrassment occurs before Allah ﷻ.

In this sense, the people who are in this real embarrassment in front of Rabbul Alamìn is mentioned with رَبَّنَا إِنَّكَ مَن تُدْخِلِ النَّارَ فَقَدْ أَخْزَيْتَهُ.

Therefore, it is important to ask constantly Allah ﷻ not to have this real embarrassment as mentioned رَبَّنَا وَآتِنَا مَا وَعَدتَّنَا عَلَى رُسُلِكَ وَلاَ تُخْزِنَا يَوْمَ الْقِيَامَةِ

The Embodiment of Hayā: Rasulullah ﷺ

It is important to understand and analyze the notion of hayā with the ayah [61] يَا أَيُّهَا الَّذِينَ آمَنُوا لَا تَدْخُلُوا بُيُوتَ النَّبِيِّ إِلَّا أَن يُؤْذَنَ لَكُمْ إِلَى طَعَامٍ غَيْرَ نَاظِرِينَ إِنَاهُ وَلَكِنْ إِذَا دُعِيتُمْ فَادْخُلُوا فَإِذَا طَعِمْتُمْ فَانتَشِرُوا وَلَا مُسْتَأْنِسِينَ لِحَدِيثٍ إِنَّ ذَلِكُمْ كَانَ يُؤْذِي النَّبِيَّ فَيَسْتَحْيِي مِنكُمْ وَاللَّهُ لَا يَسْتَحْيِي مِنَ الْحَقِّ وَإِذَا سَأَلْتُمُوهُنَّ مَتَاعًا فَاسْأَلُوهُنَّ مِن وَرَاء حِجَابٍ ذَلِكُمْ أَطْهَرُ لِقُلُوبِكُمْ وَقُلُوبِهِنَّ وَمَا كَانَ لَكُمْ أَن تُؤْذُوا رَسُولَ اللَّهِ وَلَا أَن تَنكِحُوا أَزْوَاجَهُ مِن بَعْدِهِ أَبَدًا إِنَّ ذَلِكُمْ كَانَ عِندَ اللَّهِ عَظِيمًا {الأحزاب/53}

In this regard, the Qurān mentions about the embodiment of hayā, Rasulullah ﷺ with the expression فَيَسْتَحْيِي مِنكُمْ. Having hayā from people is also a virtuous quality that one should have and maintain. Allahumma J'alna minhum, Amìn. Yet, the real hayā always should be with Allah ﷻ.

For example, not exposing the faults of couples in marriage conflicts or problems is part of this hayā. Not exposing a person's faults to others is part of this hayā. Having hayā of not doing a permissible or halāl action can be all parts of this hayā depending on the level of the person. Allahumma Ja'alna min al allazi yastahyi minka wa min-annās, Amìn.

---

61. O you who have believed, do not enter the houses of the Prophet except when you are permitted for a meal, without awaiting its readiness. But when you are invited, then enter; and when you have eaten, disperse without seeking to remain for conversation. Indeed, that [behavior] was troubling the Prophet, and he is shy of [dismissing] you. But Allah is not shy of the truth. And when you ask [his wives] for something, ask them from behind a partition. That is purer for your hearts and their hearts. And it is not [conceivable or lawful] for you to harm the Messenger of Allah or to marry his wives after him, ever. Indeed, that would be in the sight of Allah an enormity.

[195]

The Reality of Forced Migration: Diaspora

فَاسْتَجَابَ لَهُمْ رَبُّهُمْ أَنِّي لاَ أُضِيعُ عَمَلَ عَامِلٍ مِّنكُم مِّن ذَكَرٍ أَوْ أُنثَى بَعْضُكُم مِّن بَعْضٍ
فَالَّذِينَ هَاجَرُواْ وَأُخْرِجُواْ مِن دِيَارِهِمْ وَأُوذُواْ فِي سَبِيلِي وَقَاتَلُواْ وَقُتِلُواْ لأُكَفِّرَنَّ عَنْهُمْ
سَيِّئَاتِهِمْ وَلأُدْخِلَنَّهُمْ جَنَّاتٍ تَجْرِي مِن تَحْتِهَا الأَنْهَارُ ثَوَابًا مِّن عِندِ اللّهِ وَاللّهُ عِندَهُ حُسْنُ
الثَّوَابِ ٦٢ {آل عمران/195}

When analyze the ayahs of the Qurān, one of the realities that expects
the people of imān, true, justice and ethical stance is their expected and
possible destiny of the reality of their forced migration from their lands,
homes, countries and residents. The passive voice form of majhul can
indicate this forced migration of diaspora as mentioned with أُخْرِجُوا.
This is repeated in this form to indicate this forced migration in the
Qurān in different places.

The primary example of this can be witnessed in the case of
Rasulullah ﷺ from a city named as ummul qura, the mother of cities,
Makkah. Rasulullah ﷺ faced this with the sahabah (ranhum ajmain)
with difficulty, torture, social pressure and sanctions.

It is mentioned for the lives of many of the sahabahs such as
Talha Ibn Ubaydullah (ra), Zubair Ibn Awwam (Ra), Habbab Ibn Arat,
Bilal Ibn Rawaha, other asharai-mubassarah, and sahabas [8] that their
bodies were marked with the holes and injuries due their struggle of live
survivals with their imān in Allah ﷻ.

The early Muslims faced these challenges only due to their belief and
ethical stance for justice. One can also see similar cases at the time of Isa-
Jesus (as), Musa-Moses (as) and other prophets. One should remember
that this is an expected possibility for the people who struggle in this life
for the pleasure of Allah ﷻ with their imān and ethical stance for justice.

Yet, one should really remember that hijrah, or forced migration is a
test and trial that can reveal the person's or group's real disposition with

---

62. And their Lord responded to them, "Never will I allow to be lost the work of [any] worker
among you, whether male or female; you are of one another. So those who emigrated or were
evicted from their homes or were harmed in My cause or fought or were killed—I will surely
remove from them their misdeeds, and I will surely admit them to gardens beneath which
rivers flow as reward from Allah, and Allah has with Him the best reward."

وَلَوْ أَنَّا كَتَبْنَا عَلَيْهِمْ أَنِ اقْتُلُواْ أَنفُسَكُمْ أَوِ اخْرُجُواْ مِن دِيَارِكُم مَّا ⁶³ as mentioned ﷻ Allah
فَعَلُوهُ إِلاَّ قَلِيلٌ مِّنْهُمْ وَلَوْ أَنَّهُمْ فَعَلُواْ مَا يُوعَظُونَ بِهِ لَكَانَ خَيْرًا لَّهُمْ وَأَشَدَّ تَثْبِيتًا {النساء/66}.

Although the person may know this and expects these outcomes, witnessing this mass forced migration of innocent people, men, children, and women, going through different physical, emotional, and psychological difficulties, stresses and exertions can make the person spiritually devastated.

Yet, Allah ﷻ is the Most Merciful and Caring as ar-Rahman and ar-Rahim. One should always run back to Allah ﷻ for help with tawbah, and refuge in Allah ﷻ.

Hope

At this point, one can ask a lot of questions such as: "Why is this happening? Is there a way to prevent this? Was there a way to prevent this? What I can do by myself? Etc."

As we all live at a real time of presence, we are not responsible of the things that we cannot control in front of Allah ﷻ, but we are and can be responsible about what or how we can help to reduce the pain of the people going through these emotional stresses, mental and emotional breakdowns, divorces, separations with teared eyes and broken hearts.

Our initial position is and should be to give hope to the people who are going through different cycles of difficulties. Hope is directly related with Rabbul Alamin SWT as al-Rahman and al-Rahim.

Hope is directly related with imān, Islām and ihsan. Hope is directly related with order, structure, purpose, and goal of one's existence.

Hopelessness, pessimism is directly related with kufr, chaos, and disunity.

At the times of these breakdowns, giving hope as a teaching as part of the requirement of the imān is critical. Giving hope by helping them through the physical means of financial and physical support are critical as well.

Allah ﷻ mentions this reality and absolute truth of being hopeful in the Qurān. These realities and absolute truths boosting our hope is

---

63. And if We had decreed upon them, "Kill yourselves" or "Leave your homes," they would not have done it, except for a few of them. But if they had done what they were instructed, it would have been better for them and a firmer position [for them in faith].

لِأُكَفِّرَنَّ عَنْهُمْ سَيِّئَاتِهِمْ وَلِأُدْخِلَنَّهُمْ جَنَّاتٍ تَجْرِي مِن تَحْتِهَا الْأَنْهَارُ ثَوَابًا مِّن as mentioned
عِندِ اللهِ وَاللهُ عِندَهُ حُسْنُ الثَّوَابِ

The first reality of the boosting our hope is لِأُكَفِّرَنَّ عَنْهُمْ سَيِّئَاتِهِمْ. Allah ﷻ
transforms the bad deeds of the people who ever under these conditions
into the form of good deeds. This reality and absolute truth comes with
ta'kid, emphasis with Lām in لِأُكَفِّرَنَّ.

The second reality of the boosting the hope is وَلِأُدْخِلَنَّهُمْ جَنَّاتٍ تَجْرِي
مِن تَحْتِهَا الْأَنْهَارُ. Allah ﷻ will make them enter to Jannah. This reality and
absolute truth comes again with ta'kid, emphasis with waw and Lām as
in وَلِأُدْخِلَنَّهُمْ.

The third reality of the boosting hope is وَاللهُ عِندَهُ حُسْنُ الثَّوَابِ. Allah
ﷻ has all the absolute and best rewards for everyone's efforts. This is
an assurance that again comes with ta'kid of waw and with the Lafzu
Mubarak as وَاللهُ.

Sometimes, when we try to give people hope, they may think that
it is not real, but they are only ungrounded thoughts or ideas. It is just
making the person feel good. So, here hope is like a placebo drug.

SubhanAllah, here, Allah ﷻ gives assurance with ta'kid and emphasis
as an absolute truth and reality to motivate, encourage and give hope
to the person who is in depts of difficulties and trials. SubhanAllah!
Whatever promised and mentioned by Allah ﷻ is real, absolute and
perfect.

The Reality of the Need for Helping & the Diseases of our Hearts

لِلْفُقَرَاءِ الْمُهَاجِرِينَ الَّذِينَ أُخْرِجُوا مِن دِيَارِهِمْ وَأَمْوَالِهِمْ يَبْتَغُونَ فَضْلًا مِّنَ اللهِ [64]
وَرِضْوَانًا وَيَنصُرُونَ اللهَ وَرَسُولَهُ أُوْلَئِكَ هُمُ الصَّادِقُونَ {الحشر/8} وَالَّذِينَ تَبَوَّؤُوا الدَّارَ
وَالْإِيمَانَ مِن قَبْلِهِمْ يُحِبُّونَ مَنْ هَاجَرَ إِلَيْهِمْ وَلَا يَجِدُونَ فِي صُدُورِهِمْ حَاجَةً مِّمَّا أُوتُوا
وَيُؤْثِرُونَ عَلَى أَنفُسِهِمْ وَلَوْ كَانَ بِهِمْ خَصَاصَةٌ وَمَن يُوقَ شُحَّ نَفْسِهِ فَأُوْلَئِكَ هُمُ الْمُفْلِحُونَ
{الحشر/9}

---

64. For the poor emigrants who were expelled from their homes and their properties, seeking
bounty from Allah and [His] approval and supporting Allah and His Messenger, [there is
also a share]. Those are the truthful. And [also for] those who were settled in al-Madinah
and [adopted] the faith before them. They love those who emigrated to them and find not
any want in their breasts of what the emigrants were given but give [them] preference over
themselves, even though they are in privation. And whoever is protected from the stinginess
of his soul—it is those who will be the successful.

It is important to realize the reality of the need of these people leaving their lands, homes, and countries due to the reasons of forced migration. They need different livelihood means to survive and adapt spiritually and physically flourish with the new openings as Allah ﷻ can grant.

In this reality of helping, the people who realizes this influx of people should do their utmost effort of helping them.

The influx of people coming are referred as muhajirûn. The locals are called ansâr.

In the efforts of helping of ansâr for the people of muhajirûn, ansâr should be in the state of natural, happy and content state of helping these muhajirûn. There should not be any ill feelings in these engagements of helping efforts as mentioned وَلَا يَجِدُونَ فِي صُدُورِهِمْ حَاجَةً مِّمَّا أُوتُوا.

This engagement of helping to muhajirûn should be in such a state and way that the ansâr should do sacrifice, go above and beyond in their helping efforts even if it puts the muhajirûn in difficulty of changing their routine life styles as mentioned وَيُؤْثِرُونَ عَلَى أَنفُسِهِمْ وَلَوْ كَانَ بِهِمْ خَصَاصَةٌ.

One should understand that when we are helping each other, our nafs often engage in the self-dialogue of selfish attitudes such as: "Why are you helping? Isn't there any other person to help them? Why do we need to destroy our routine? Can't there be any other possibility? I think, these people don't need any help. They can survive on their own."

Above are some examples of the self-dialogue of the selfish and raw nafs that one should be aware of. Even if these thoughts come to the person, one should take all the efforts and means to detach and isolate oneself from these thoughts with istigfar and asking help, 'ianah from Allah ﷻ.

The expression شُحَّ نَفْسِهِ can indicate these self-engagements of the nafs as a self-dialogue similar to above thoughts.

Yet, one should remember if the person is successful in achieving these isolation and detachment of oneself from these notions of شُحَّ نَفْسِهِ, then there is a promise from Allah ﷻ as mentioned فَأُوْلَٰئِكَ هُمُ الْمُفْلِحُونَ. These are both spiritual and physical openings and victories for the person.

Allahumma J'aalna Minhum, Amìn

اللَّهُمَّ جَعَلْنَا مِنهُم ، آمين

The Nature of the People of Forced Migration

When we study the Qurān about the nature of these muhajirūn forced for migration, one can realize some of their qualities.

One of their quality is that they are following the guidelines as established by Allah ﷻ and all the prophets as part of the sunnah. These guidelines when followed can reveal the natural state of a human being called as fitrah. In this sense, these guidelines are pure, natural and fit in the natural, fitri human creation as instructed by Allah ﷻ.

This is mentioned as [65] فَمَا كَانَ جَوَابَ قَوْمِهِ إِلَّا أَن قَالُوا أَخْرِجُوا آلَ لُوطٍ مِّن قَرْيَتِكُمْ إِنَّهُمْ أُنَاسٌ يَتَطَهَّرُونَ {النمل/56}

In this regard, there were, are and will be people in societies who want to follow and teach themselves from these natural teachings as instructed by Allah ﷻ. Yet, the ones who still want to abide and teach these natural teachings of Allah ﷻ and Rasulullah ﷺ and other prophets as mentioned إِنَّهُمْ أُنَاسٌ يَتَطَهَّرُونَ would be often forced to leave their land or countries as mentioned أَخْرِجُوا.

It is interesting to realize that the people who oppress and do the zulm of forcing the people to leave their own habitat accept that these people are the people of justice, fairness, solidarity, objectivity, and purity as mentioned إِنَّهُمْ أُنَاسٌ يَتَطَهَّرُونَ.

One can now remember exactly the same expressions in the history by the opponents of Rasulullah ﷺ and sahabah when they were forced to leave makkah similar to the people of Lut as in this ayah.

One can also measure the quality of the people in today's forced migrations in Muslim societies if today's modern muhajirūn have the same quality of following the fitri and natural states of following the Qurān and sunnah of Rasulullah ﷺ.

If these are accepted and uttered by the opponents of these modern muhajirūn, then both modern muhajirūn and ansār should say Alhamdulillah that they fit in the Qurānic pattern as described in this ayah as mentioned إِنَّهُمْ أُنَاسٌ يَتَطَهَّرُونَ.

سبحان الله وبحمده،استغفرك و اتوب اليك

SubhanAllahu wa Bihamdihi, Astagfiruka wa attubu ilayk.

---

65. But the answer of his people was not except that they said, "Expel the family of Lot from your city. Indeed, they are people who keep themselves pure."

Re-Establishment after the Forced Migration

One should remember that it is important to reestablish oneself as an individual, family and society after the cases of forced migration. In other words, as our life is short. Migration, hijrah is one of the noble practices that Rasulullah ﷺ did and we are willingly or unwillingly following this sunnah with the Fadl and Rahmah of Allah ﷻ.

Yet, we should look and prioritize our steps in the re-establishment period in our new lives as muhajirûn and ansâr for our newly engagements.

One can review the ayahs as [66] أُذِنَ لِلَّذِينَ يُقَاتَلُونَ بِأَنَّهُمْ ظُلِمُوا وَإِنَّ اللَّهَ عَلَى نَصْرِهِمْ لَقَدِيرٌ {الحج/39} الَّذِينَ أُخْرِجُوا مِن دِيَارِهِم بِغَيْرِ حَقٍّ إِلَّا أَن يَقُولُوا رَبُّنَا اللَّهُ وَلَوْلَا دَفْعُ اللَّهِ النَّاسَ بَعْضَهُم بِبَعْضٍ لَّهُدِّمَتْ صَوَامِعُ وَبِيَعٌ وَصَلَوَاتٌ وَمَسَاجِدُ يُذْكَرُ فِيهَا اسْمُ اللَّهِ كَثِيرًا وَلَيَنصُرَنَّ اللَّهُ مَن يَنصُرُهُ إِنَّ اللَّهَ لَقَوِيٌّ عَزِيزٌ {الحج/40} الَّذِينَ إِن مَّكَّنَّاهُمْ فِي الْأَرْضِ أَقَامُوا الصَّلَاةَ وَآتَوُا الزَّكَاةَ وَأَمَرُوا بِالْمَعْرُوفِ وَنَهَوْا عَنِ الْمُنكَرِ وَلِلَّهِ عَاقِبَةُ الْأُمُورِ {الحج/41}

It is interesting to realize that after recollecting oneself as an individual, family or group as mentioned أُذِنَ لِلَّذِينَ يُقَاتَلُونَ بِأَنَّهُمْ ظُلِمُوا, there can be order of steps to follow.

The first is possibly to establish a place of worship, masjid, in this new habitat or land as one's real and primary purpose of life in their relation with Rabbul Alamìn through 'ibadah and other affairs as mentioned صَوَامِعُ وَبِيَعٌ وَصَلَوَاتٌ وَمَسَاجِدُ يُذْكَرُ فِيهَا اسْمُ اللَّهِ كَثِيرًا. Yet, in this primary established institution, everyone needs a collective encouragement of remembering Allah ﷻ, much dhikr as mentioned وَمَسَاجِدُ يُذْكَرُ فِيهَا اسْمُ اللَّهِ كَثِيرًا.

Abudance of Dhikr and remembrance of Allah ﷻ will solve almost all the spiritual and physical problems with the inayah, Fadl and Rahmah of Allah ﷻ. So, ensuring the institutions to establish this primary and essential existential goal of Dhikrullah in abundant quantity is very but very critical.

Without the dhikr and remembrance of Allah ﷻ, all other efforts will be meaningless, less motivating and people will not be recovered from

---

66. Permission [to fight] has been given to those who are being fought, because they were wronged. And indeed, Allah is competent to give them victory. Permission [to fight] has been given to those who are being fought, because they were wronged. And indeed, Allah is competent to give them victory. [And they are] those who, if We give them authority in the land, establish prayer and give zakah and enjoin what is right and forbid what is wrong. And to Allah belongs the outcome of [all] matters.

their past, present and future related spiritual disturbances, diseases and worries.

Along with this primary goal of Dhikrullah in abundant quantities in the embodiment of salāh through institutions such as masājid, then other responsibilities can follow as الَّذِينَ إِن مَّكَّنَّاهُمْ فِي الْأَرْضِ أَقَامُوا الصَّلَاةَ وَآتَوُا الزَّكَاةَ. These are وَآتَوُا الزَّكَاةَ وَأَمَرُوا بِالْمَعْرُوفِ وَنَهَوْا عَنِ الْمُنكَرِ وَلِلَّهِ عَاقِبَةُ الْأُمُورِ. وَأَمَرُوا بِالْمَعْرُوفِ وَنَهَوْا عَنِ الْمُنكَرِ.

After these forced migrations, financial institutions, helping others, ensuring justice and ethical behavior and other are all critical in this new venue of land as mentioned إِن مَّكَّنَّاهُمْ فِي الْأَرْضِ.

Further Steps of Etiquettes and Diplomacy after Re-establishment

One should remember after the re-establishment, one should use their experience of past difficulties in order not to retaliate but still maintain justice, fairness and ethical behavior in their new land.

One can analyze the ayahs in this perspective as [67] لَا يَنْهَاكُمُ اللَّهُ عَنِ الَّذِينَ لَمْ يُقَاتِلُوكُمْ فِي الدِّينِ وَلَمْ يُخْرِجُوكُم مِّن دِيَارِكُمْ أَن تَبَرُّوهُمْ وَتُقْسِطُوا إِلَيْهِمْ إِنَّ اللَّهَ يُحِبُّ الْمُقْسِطِينَ {الممتحنة/8} إِنَّمَا يَنْهَاكُمُ اللَّهُ عَنِ الَّذِينَ قَاتَلُوكُمْ فِي الدِّينِ وَأَخْرَجُوكُم مِّن دِيَارِكُمْ وَظَاهَرُوا عَلَى إِخْرَاجِكُمْ أَن تَوَلَّوْهُمْ وَمَن يَتَوَلَّهُمْ فَأُولَٰئِكَ هُمُ الظَّالِمُونَ {الممتحنة/9} يَا أَيُّهَا الَّذِينَ آمَنُوا إِذَا جَاءَكُمُ الْمُؤْمِنَاتُ مُهَاجِرَاتٍ فَامْتَحِنُوهُنَّ اللَّهُ أَعْلَمُ بِإِيمَانِهِنَّ فَإِنْ عَلِمْتُمُوهُنَّ مُؤْمِنَاتٍ فَلَا تَرْجِعُوهُنَّ إِلَى الْكُفَّارِ لَا هُنَّ حِلٌّ لَّهُمْ وَلَا هُمْ يَحِلُّونَ لَهُنَّ وَآتُوهُم مَّا أَنفَقُوا وَلَا جُنَاحَ عَلَيْكُمْ أَن تَنكِحُوهُنَّ إِذَا آتَيْتُمُوهُنَّ أُجُورَهُنَّ وَلَا تُمْسِكُوا بِعِصَمِ الْكَوَافِرِ وَاسْأَلُوا مَا أَنفَقْتُمْ وَلْيَسْأَلُوا مَا أَنفَقُوا ذَٰلِكُمْ حُكْمُ اللَّهِ يَحْكُمُ بَيْنَكُمْ وَاللَّهُ عَلِيمٌ حَكِيمٌ {الممتحنة/10}.

In any land, and especially in the new land of migration, regardless of the people's beliefs, culture and system, one should maintain justice, fairness, appreciation, and solidarity with the people as mentioned in

---

67. Allah does not forbid you from those who do not fight you because of religion and do not expel you from your homes—from being righteous toward them and acting justly toward them. Indeed, Allah loves those who act justly. Allah only forbids you from those who fight you because of religion and expel you from your homes and aid in your expulsion—[forbids] that you make allies of them. And whoever makes allies of them, then it is those who are the wrongdoers. O you who have believed, when the believing women come to you as emigrants, examine them. Allah is most knowing as to their faith. And if you know them to be believers, then do not return them to the disbelievers; they are not lawful [wives] for them, nor are they lawful [husbands] for them. But give the disbelievers what they have spent. And there is no blame upon you if you marry them when you have given them their due compensation. And hold not to marriage bonds with disbelieving women, but ask for what you have spent and let them ask for what they have spent. That is the judgement of Allah; He judges between you. And Allah is Knowing and Wise.

لَا يَنْهَاكُمُ أَللَّهُ عَنِ الَّذِينَ لَمْ يُقَاتِلُوكُمْ فِي الدِّينِ وَلَمْ يُخْرِجُوكُم مِّن دِيَارِكُمْ أَن تَبَرُّوهُمْ the ayah [68]
وَتُقْسِطُوا إِلَيْهِمْ إِنَّ اللَّهَ يُحِبُّ الْمُقْسِطِينَ {الممتحنة/8}.

There is an encouragement by Allah ﷻ to be the people of justice, and fairness as mentioned with the word adalah and qist mentioned as وَتُقْسِطُوا إِلَيْهِمْ إِنَّ اللَّهَ يُحِبُّ الْمُقْسِطِينَ {الممتحنة/8}.

One should remember that the people who were the oppressors, helping the oppressors, and forcing the people to leave their habitat, homes and residence are the ones against justice and fairness.

Yet, Rasulullah ﷺ displayed an embodiment of forgiveness in his life time and even when he ﷺ returned to Makkah to conquer this city. He ﷺ forgave and showed the natural disposition of forgiveness in the powerful position of retaliating to the people who had used all the means to oppress and torture the Muslims due to their beliefs.

This was the exemplary position of Rasulullah ﷺ. This was the position of other anbiya such as Yusuf as in the same position of authority as [69] قَالَ لَا تَثْرِيبَ عَلَيْكُمُ الْيَوْمَ يَغْفِرُ أَللَّهُ لَكُمْ وَهُوَ أَرْحَمُ الرَّاحِمِينَ {يوسف/29}.

One should remember that during this influx of forced migrations and re-establishments, there will be always the cases and people who would try to take advantage of these situations and possibly have different and wrong intentions.

In this regard, the ayah mentions this reality as يَا أَيُّهَا الَّذِينَ آمَنُوا إِذَا جَاءَكُمُ الْمُؤْمِنَاتُ مُهَاجِرَاتٍ فَامْتَحِنُوهُنَّ اللَّهُ أَعْلَمُ بِإِيمَانِهِنَّ. Yet, even in this situations, it is important to follow a proper etiquette and diplomacy or protocol as فَامْتَحِنُوهُنَّ اللَّهُ أَعْلَمُ بِإِيمَانِهِنَّ فَإِنْ عَلِمْتُمُوهُنَّ مُؤْمِنَاتٍ فَلَا تَرْجِعُوهُنَّ إِلَى الْكُفَّارِ mentioned لَا هُنَّ حِلٌّ لَّهُمْ وَلَا هُمْ يَحِلُّونَ لَهُنَّ وَآتُوهُم مَّا أَنفَقُوا.

---

68. Allah does not forbid you from those who do not fight you because of religion and do not expel you from your homes—from being righteous toward them and acting justly toward them. Indeed, Allah loves those who act justly.

69. He said, "No blame will there be upon you today. Allah will forgive you; and He is the most merciful of the merciful."

Juz 6

Sûrah 4 -Al-Nisã

[103]

فَإِذَا قَضَيْتُمُ الصَّلَاةَ فَاذْكُرُواْ اللَّهَ قِيَامًا وَقُعُودًا وَعَلَى جُنُوبِكُمْ فَإِذَا اطْمَأْنَنتُمْ فَأَقِيمُواْ الصَّلَاةَ
إِنَّ الصَّلَاةَ كَانَتْ عَلَى الْمُؤْمِنِينَ كِتَابًا ⁷⁰ مَّوْقُوتًا {النساء/103}

One should remember that salah is the essence and seed of all 'ibadah.
As humans is the essence of the universe, and Sûrah Fatiha is the essence
of the Qurãn, salah is the core of all 'ibadah. One can understand this
critical position of salah among all other 'ibadahs with the expression إِنَّ
الصَّلَاةَ كَانَتْ عَلَى الْمُؤْمِنِينَ كِتَابًا مَّوْقُوتًا.

[148-149]

لاَّ يُحِبُّ اللّهُ الْجَهْرَ بِالسُّوَءِ مِنَ الْقَوْلِ إِلاَّ مَن ظُلِمَ وَكَانَ اللّهُ سَمِيعًا عَلِيمًا {النساء/148}
إِن تُبْدُواْ خَيْرًا أَوْ تُخْفُوهُ أَوْ تَعْفُواْ عَن سُوَءٍ ⁷¹ فَإِنَّ اللّهَ كَانَ عَفُوًّا قَدِيرًا {النساء/149}

It is important not to be belligerent, rude, and intimidating in language
especially at the times of anger leading to possible verbal abuse in
argumentation and quarrels. This may especially happen in family
matters of husband and wife relationships, or parent and children
relationships.

The true authority requires when there is the means to take revenge
that one still should and can act in composure and calmness in decision
making and even in the display of facial and verbal and physical
dispositions.

---

70. And when you are among them and lead them in prayer, let a group of them stand [in
prayer] with you and let them carry their arms. And when they have prostrated, let them be
[in position] behind you and have the other group come forward which has not [yet] prayed
and let them pray with you, taking precaution and carrying their arms. Those who disbelieve
wish that you would neglect your weapons and your baggage so they could come down
upon you in one [single] attack. But there is no blame upon you, if you are troubled by rain
or are ill, for putting down your arms, but take precaution. Indeed, Allah has prepared for the
disbelievers a humiliating punishment.
71. Allah does not like the public mention of evil except by one who has been wronged. And
ever is Allah Hearing and Knowing. If [instead] you show [some] good or conceal it or pardon
an offense—indeed, Allah is ever Pardoning and Competent.

As it is mentioned with الْجَهْرَ بِالسُّوءِ مِنَ الْقَوْلِ, the bad and heart-breaking words and statements can lead to the displeasure of Allah ﷻ. May Allah ﷻ protect us from our own evil nafs, Amìn!

One can realize that إِلَّا مَن ظُلِمَ is a condition. Yet, even in these conditional allowances, the better disposition to move on and not take it personally and forget it as mentioned إِن تُبْدُواْ خَيْرًا أَوْ تُخْفُوهُ أَوْ تَعْفُواْ عَن سُوَءٍ فَإِنَّ اللّهَ كَانَ عَفُوًّا قَدِيرًا {النساء/149}.

All humans have the natural tendencies to expose the faults of others due to their evil-renderings of nafs and ego. Yet, if one wants to be different as to be close to Allah ﷻ, then one should follow the general tendencies of the nafs like everyone but put a thick skin of insensitivity against people's verbal and facial related abuses, move on and forget, and forgive.

Because, our main goal in this life to retract the people's lost imān. We should not be sidetracked about the minute and secondary means, effects or causes. If we are walking on a path to reach a goal, and if there are things trying to pull us on the side, we will still try and struggle to walk on the path to finish a goal oriented journey as our logic and reason would dictate.

Yet, when there are overpowering emotions, the person may know the logical stance but yet can act with emotions and lose again at the end although he or she may know this bad repeated consequence. At these times and at all times, one should constantly refuge in Allah ﷻ with istigfar, salah, dhikr, recitation of Qurān and even if one is going to change environment changing it without others knowing the real reason of it can be very critical to restrain one's emotions and overpower the situation with reason and logic.

One should really but really remember, understand and embody the disposition that "Even though, I can be in good peaceful states of imān now with sakina, confidence and certainty of haqq and truth, yet I do not have any guarantee for the next one second or minute that I won't lose myself and destroy myself, and the people around me if there is no 'iana, help of Allah ﷻ.

اللّهم جَعَلنا مِن الذين "لا تكلني الى نفس طرفت عيّن" آمين

Allahumma Ja'alna Min Allazina "La Takilni ila nafsin tarfata a'ynin" Amìn.

Sûrah 5 al-Maida

[32]

مِنْ أَجْلِ ذَلِكَ كَتَبْنَا عَلَى بَني إِسْرَائِيلَ أَنَّهُ مَن قَتَلَ نَفْسًا بِغَيْرِ نَفْسٍ أَوْ فَسَادٍ فِي الأَرْضِ
فَكَأَنَّمَا قَتَلَ النَّاسَ جَمِيعًا وَمَنْ أَحْيَاهَا ٧٢ فَكَأَنَّمَا أَحْيَا النَّاسَ جَمِيعًا وَلَقَدْ جَاء تْهُمْ رُسُلُنَا
بِالْبَيِّنَاتِ ثُمَّ إِنَّ كَثِيرًا مِّنْهُم بَعْدَ ذَلِكَ فِي الأَرْضِ لَمُسْرِفُونَ {المائدة/32}

One should remember that there are two types of killings and revivals. One is the physical and the other is the spiritual.

In the case of physical killing, it all agreed anonymously that Allah ﷻ does not give permission people to kill others. In the case of physical revival, Allah ﷻ is the One who gives life. There can be the miracles that Allah ﷻ enabled some to show the reflection of this revival.

The other case is spiritual killing and revival. This may apply to all of us in our different positions and roles in life.

Pessimism, distrust, cynicism, negativity, suspicion, gloominess, hopelessness, laziness, discouragement, devaluation, mockery and humiliating of others, unconstructiveness, skepticism, disapproval, opposition, quarrels, chaos, anger, stress, anxiety, disorder, purposelessness, and arguments lead to spiritual killing.

Hope, optimism, trust, faith, encouragement, approval, firmness, agreement, hard work, regularity, predictability, structure, order, stability, calmness, serenity, composure, tranquility, self-control, certainty, meaning, valuation, purpose, goal, motivation, consent, and harmony lead to spiritual revival.

There are many examples of this in life. If one gives confidence of encouragement to their children, then he or she will be motivated to work and try hard. The opposite is true as well.

---

72. And do not wish for that by which Allah has made some of you exceed others. For men is a share of what they have earned, and for women is a share of what they have earned. And ask Allah of his bounty. Indeed Allah is ever, of all things, Knowing.

Juz 8

Sûrah 7 al-A'râf

[26-27]

يَا بَنِي آدَمَ قَدْ أَنزَلْنَا عَلَيْكُمْ لِبَاسًا يُوَارِي سَوْءَاتِكُمْ وَرِيشًا وَلِبَاسُ التَّقْوَىٰ ذَٰلِكَ خَيْرٌ ذَٰلِكَ
مِنْ آيَاتِ اللَّهِ لَعَلَّهُمْ يَذَّكَّرُونَ 73 {الأعراف/26} يَا بَنِي آدَمَ لَا يَفْتِنَنَّكُمُ الشَّيْطَانُ كَمَا أَخْرَجَ
أَبَوَيْكُم مِّنَ الْجَنَّةِ يَنزِعُ عَنْهُمَا لِبَاسَهُمَا لِيُرِيَهُمَا سَوْءَاتِهِمَا إِنَّهُ يَرَاكُمْ هُوَ وَقَبِيلُهُ مِنْ حَيْثُ
لَا تَرَوْنَهُمْ إِنَّا جَعَلْنَا الشَّيَاطِينَ أَوْلِيَاءَ لِلَّذِينَ لَا يُؤْمِنُونَ {الأعراف/27}

One can consider the hikmah of libās, dress for humans compared to other creation. Allah ﷻ has given all the animals a natural dress that they have it with their original creation. Some animals have furry. Some have certain leathers. Some have certain skins.

Yet, humans have the choice of deciding what to wear and when to wear. In this sense, the word أَنزَلْنَا in the expression يَا بَنِي آدَمَ قَدْ أَنزَلْنَا عَلَيْكُمْ لِبَاسًا shows this unique position of humans in dress selection and choice [1] [2].

When one reviews sabab-nuzûl of this ayah, one can find early practices of people before Islām making tawaf of Kabah naked [3]. In this regard, this ayah displays an urge to remove this false custom with Islām and embody modesty, haya by covering themselves. Therefore, one can find detailed descriptions in fiqh about the limits of awrah for man and woman that requires covering with the Divine law. These fiqh laws are all the required externalities of modesty, haya with people and with truly Allah ﷻ. Although Allah ﷻ is aware one's all internalities and externalities as our Creator, our Rabb, the implementations of externalities such as dress as outlined by Allah ﷻ can instill us the true embodiment of haya, modesty, or taqwa with Allah ﷻ primarily. Then, as the reflection of this embodiment, one can find haya, modesty or taqwa with others.

---

73. O children of Adam, We have bestowed upon you clothing to conceal your private parts and as adornment. But the clothing of righteousness—that is best. That is from the signs of Allah that perhaps they will remember. O children of Adam, let not Satan tempt you as he removed your parents from Paradise, stripping them of their clothing to show them their private parts. Indeed, he sees you, he and his tribe, from where you do not see them. Indeed, We have made the devils allies to those who do not believe.

When we review the second part of the ayah the expression وَلِبَاسُ
التَّقْوَىٰ ذَٰلِكَ can reveal spiritual body to wear the dress of taqwa as Imam
Kushayri can indicate [10].

With this perspective, when we look at the relations between humans
among each other and humans relation with Allah ﷻ , the teachings of
taqwa are expected.

The portion of the ayah as يَنزِعُ عَنْهُمَا لِبَاسَهُمَا لِيُرِيَهُمَا سَوْءَاتِهِمَا can be
an example for the application of taqwa among humans. In this regard,
taqwa can be a definition of personal boundaries as outlined by Allah
ﷻ that the person does not transgress and goes limits or personal
boundaries of another human being, or creation.

In other words, everyone is a personal space with its boundaries
given by Allah ﷻ. This personal space of the person deserves respect.
No one can transgress this personal space of the person that is given by
Allah ﷻ. In this regard, making choice, freedom of expression, freedom
to live are all part of this personal space. Allah ﷻ is the ultimate Judge
of everyone in the afterlife for the choice and usage of these personal
spaces. This judgment is not our responsibility as humans.

Taqwa requires to recognize these personal spaces of all living
creation giving by by Allah ﷻ. Taqwa requires recognition and not
transgression into other's personal spaces.

Absence of taqwa can lead to transgression into personal spaces.
These transgressions can lead into chaos, fithnah, and disunity among
individuals, family members and societies.

When we look at the most detrimental chaos in a unit is the case of
separation or divorce among couples. This end product of divorce entails
the prior engagements of transgressions or abuse. These transgressions
or abuse entails entering into innate right of the personal spaces given
by Allah ﷻ. This transgression into personal spaces is due to the absence
of taqwa in individuals.

Each argumentation, dispute or breaking one's heart is a step and an
indicator for partial or full absence of taqwa when one transgresses into
the personal space of another person.

One should remember that we try to outline our social and familial
interactions with the value system that is given to us by Allah ﷻ. Yet,
there are bare minimums that each individual has a right innately by
birth given by Allah ﷻ. These are choice, existence, and respect. There
is no force in religion. There is no force in choice or decision making.

One should remember that if one wants to follow the teachings of the Qurān and Sunnah, it is expected that he or she outlines their behavior, engagements, responsibilities and decision makings in this value system. Yet, whether he does it or not, each person's individual accountability is with Allah ﷻ. It is not with other humans such as husbands, wives, parents, teachers, friends, or society.

The punishment system in Islamic legal system is based on the cases of transgressions of individual rights. In this regard, publicizing trasgression in order to promote a transgression is also considered a transgression for the individual rights of others in that society. Yet, if any sin is not publicized or promoted that is related with the individual then, there is no right of the institution to reveal the faults of others. One can remember the case of Omar ra with a drunk a person [11] (hadith #: 8198).

Today, one can also view accepting each person's right of the personal space as a way of professional relationship in today's popular terms. In this regard, although this phrase may not be fully appropriate, a person may need to have a professional relationship with their spouses, children, parents similar to his or her coworkers at workplace.

Traditionally, the concept of professionalism has been referred as adab in our rich Islamic history. In this regard, our positions require an adab with each individual in different expected manners. Yet, at the end, the ultimate source of taqwa is due to the required adab with Allah ﷻ. Our different positions of having taqwa, professionalism or adab all stem from this primary required adab with Allah ﷻ. Although others may claim other value systems, absence of the true adab with Allah ﷻ negates and nullifies and invalidates all the other false value systems.

True adab with Allah ﷻ is in the Qurān and in the Hadith as embodied by Rasulullah ﷺ. Yes, the primary embodiment of adab with Allah ﷻ is Rasulullah ﷺ. Therefore, all the teachings of Rasulullah ﷺ related with adab is primary.

One should remember that taqwa requires us not to transgress into the personal space of other humans and all creation. The primary goal of Shaytān is to instigate us to go to the personal spaces of others. Shaytān with his army work so hard on us by analyzing our characters, weaknesses and tendencies in order to infiltrate into our thoughts giving ideas so that we can make verbal or physical choices, actions and/or executions to transgress into the personal spaces of others.

The primary struggle and focus of Shaytān to ensure chaos, disunity and fitnah in societies is to break the unity among couples between husband and wife as mentioned in the hadith [7] (hadith # 2813). If divorce is achieved, then all the individuals related in this relationship such as husband, wife, children, and even all the society made of from these family units, will be in shattered states of heart and mind.

When people are in the shattered states of heart and mind, then people cannot focus. La ilaha illa Allah requires focus. Tawhid is the opposite of multiplicity. Each multiplicity for humans is a source of distraction. Divorce is the main source of distraction for all the affected individuals in the relationship.

In this regard, any effort, argument or dispute that can prepare and invest for the outcome of divorce among couples can be a sign of loss of taqwa on the part of individuals. This loss is an achievement on the part of Shaytān.

Now, one can analyze the portions of the ayah [74] كَمَا لَا يَفْتِنَنَّكُمُ الشَّيْطَانُ أَخْرَجَ أَبَوَيْكُم مِّنَ الْجَنَّةِ يَنزِعُ عَنْهُمَا لِبَاسَهُمَا لِيُرِيَهُمَا سَوْءَاتِهِمَا إِنَّهُ يَرَاكُمْ هُوَ وَقَبِيلُهُ مِنْ حَيْثُ لاَ تَرَوْنَهُمْ إِنَّا جَعَلْنَا الشَّيَاطِينَ أَوْلِيَاء لِلَّذِينَ لاَ يُؤْمِنُونَ {الأعراف/72}

In this regard, the word libās in the ayah يَنزِعُ عَنْهُمَا لِبَاسَهُمَا لِيُرِيَهُمَا سَوْءَاتِهِمَا can indicate the limits of personal space of each individual with externalities that entail taqwa so that the person should not transgress. When people, or couples argue, they can transgress into the personal space of another, especially as they try to expose their faults with the absence of taqwa as mentioned لِيُرِيَهُمَا سَوْءَاتِهِمَا.

At the end, the instigator works so hard as mentioned لاَ يَفْتِنَنَّكُمُ الشَّيْطَانُ or إِنَّهُ يَرَاكُمْ هُوَ وَقَبِيلُهُ مِنْ حَيْثُ لاَ تَرَوْنَهُمْ إِنَّا. Even they get the support of other Shaytān in the human forms who do not have the taqwa, fear or value sytem of the Qurān and Sunnah as mentioned إِنَّا جَعَلْنَا الشَّيَاطِينَ أَوْلِيَاء لِلَّذِينَ لاَ يُؤْمِنُونَ.

When the believers argue and when they are in dispute, then they lose their strength and their ni'mahs that Allah ﷻ gave them due to their struggle of keeping the unity of family, Jam'ah, or society. This is mentioned here as كَمَا أَخْرَجَ أَبَوَيْكُم مِّنَ الْجَنَّةِ

---

74. O children of Adam, let not Satan tempt you as he removed your parents from Paradise, stripping them of their clothing to show them their private parts. Indeed, he sees you, he and his tribe, from where you do not see them. Indeed, We have made the devils allies to those who do not believe.

It is also mentioned in other parts of the Qurān as: [75]

وَأَطِيعُوا اللَّهَ وَرَسُولَهُ وَلاَ تَنَازَعُوا فَتَفْشَلُوا وَتَذْهَبَ رِيحُكُمْ وَاصْبِرُوا إِنَّ اللَّهَ مَعَ الصَّابِرِينَ
{الأنفال/46}

When we forgive, don't see the faults of others and make shukr to Allah ﷻ in every state regardless of evil or good looking, then Allah ﷻ increases the ni'mahs on us. Allahumma J'alna minhum, Amīn. This is mentioned in many places in the Qurān as

يَا أَيُّهَا الَّذِينَ آمَنُوا إِنَّ مِنْ أَزْوَاجِكُمْ وَأَوْلَادِكُمْ عَدُوًّا لَّكُمْ فَاحْذَرُوهُمْ وَإِن تَعْفُوا وَتَصْفَحُوا [76]
وَتَغْفِرُوا فَإِنَّ اللَّهَ غَفُورٌ رَّحِيمٌ {التغابن/14}

فَتَبَسَّمَ ضَاحِكًا مِّن قَوْلِهَا وَقَالَ رَبِّ أَوْزِعْنِي أَنْ أَشْكُرَ نِعْمَتَكَ الَّتِي أَنْعَمْتَ عَلَيَّ وَعَلَى
وَالِدَيَّ وَأَنْ أَعْمَلَ صَالِحًا تَرْضَاهُ وَأَدْخِلْنِي بِرَحْمَتِكَ فِي عِبَادِكَ الصَّالِحِينَ {النمل/19}

وَإِذْ تَأَذَّنَ رَبُّكُمْ لَئِن شَكَرْتُمْ لأَزِيدَنَّكُمْ وَلَئِن كَفَرْتُمْ إِنَّ عَذَابِي لَشَدِيدٌ {إبراهيم/7}

Therefore, libās requires taqwa. Taqwa in the form of libās requires not transgressing into the personal space of others. Personal space of each individual can entail their mistakes, faults or sins. Yet, taqwa of libās requires not exposing faults of others when one knows them. True taqwa of libās requires even not recognizing the faults of others but focusing on their own faults.

The manifestation of libas of taqwa display and emerge in human relations. This is not a theoretical concept but it is in everyday life in our all familial, social and humanly relations.

The primary manifestation of this libas of taqwa is between the couples. In this relation, the individuals constantly spend time with each other. They constantly see each other's faults. If libas of taqwa is not present, the relationships do not last and will not exist.

---

75. And between them will be a partition, and on [its] elevations are men who recognize all by their mark. And they call out to the companions of Paradise, "Peace be upon you." They have not [yet] entered it, but they long intensely.

76. O you who have believed, indeed, among your wives and your children are enemies to you, so beware of them. But if you pardon and overlook and forgive—then indeed, Allah is Forgiving and Merciful. So [Solomon] smiled, amused at her speech, and said, "My Lord, enable me to be grateful for Your favor which You have bestowed upon me and upon my parents and to do righteousness of which You approve. And admit me by Your mercy into [the ranks of] Your righteous servants." And [remember] when your Lord proclaimed, 'If you are grateful, I will surely increase you [in favor]; but if you deny, indeed, My punishment is severe.'"

It is interesting realize that the Qurān emphasizes the couple relationships with the word libās as mentioned

أُحِلَّ لَكُمْ لَيْلَةَ الصِّيَامِ الرَّفَثُ إِلَى نِسَائِكُمْ هُنَّ لِبَاسٌ لَكُمْ وَأَنتُمْ لِبَاسٌ لَهُنَّ عَلِمَ اللهُ أَنَّكُمْ ⁷⁷

كُنتُمْ تَخْتانُونَ أَنفُسَكُمْ فَتَابَ عَلَيْكُمْ وَعَفَا عَنكُمْ فَالآنَ بَاشِرُوهُنَّ وَابْتَغُواْ مَا كَتَبَ اللهُ لَكُمْ

وَكُلُواْ وَاشْرَبُواْ حَتَّى يَتَبَيَّنَ لَكُمُ الْخَيْطُ الأَبْيَضُ مِنَ الْخَيْطِ الأَسْوَدِ مِنَ الْفَجْرِ ثُمَّ أَتِمُواْ

الصِّيَامَ إِلَى الَّليْلِ وَلاَ تُبَاشِرُوهُنَّ وَأَنتُمْ عَاكِفُونَ فِي الْمَسَاجِدِ تِلْكَ حُدُودُ اللهِ فَلاَ تَقْرَبُوهَا

كَذَلِكَ يُبَيِّنُ اللهُ آيَاتِهِ لِلنَّاسِ لَعَلَّهُمْ يَتَّقُونَ {البقرة/187}

Juz 10

Sûrah 9 Al-Tawbah

[38-40]

Works of Deen & Motivation

يَا أَيُّهَا الَّذِينَ آمَنُواْ مَا لَكُمْ إِذَا قِيلَ لَكُمُ انفِرُواْ فِي سَبِيلِ اللهِ اثَّاقَلْتُمْ إِلَى الأَرْضِ أَرَضِيتُم ⁷⁸

بِالْحَيَاةِ الدُّنْيَا مِنَ الآخِرَةِ فَمَا مَتَاعُ الْحَيَاةِ الدُّنْيَا فِي الآخِرَةِ إِلاَّ قَلِيلٌ {التوبة/38} إِلاَّ

تَنفِرُواْ يُعَذِّبْكُمْ عَذَابًا أَلِيمًا وَيَسْتَبْدِلْ قَوْمًا غَيْرَكُمْ وَلاَ تَضُرُّوهُ شَيْئًا وَاللهُ عَلَى كُلِّ شَيْءٍ

قَدِيرٌ {التوبة/39} إِلاَّ تَنصُرُوهُ فَقَدْ نَصَرَهُ اللهُ إِذْ أَخْرَجَهُ الَّذِينَ كَفَرُواْ ثَانِيَ اثْنَيْنِ إِذْ

هُمَا فِي الْغَارِ إِذْ يَقُولُ لِصَاحِبِهِ لاَ تَحْزَنْ إِنَّ اللهَ مَعَنَا فَأَنزَلَ اللهُ سَكِينَتَهُ عَلَيْهِ وَأَيَّدَهُ

بِجُنُودٍ لَّمْ تَرَوْهَا وَجَعَلَ كَلِمَةَ الَّذِينَ كَفَرُواْ السُّفْلَى وَكَلِمَةُ اللهِ هِيَ الْعُلْيَا وَاللهُ عَزِيزٌ حَكِيمٌ

{التوبة/40}

---

77. It has been made permissible for you the night preceding fasting to go to your wives [for sexual relations]. They are clothing for you and you are clothing for them. Allah knows that you used to deceive yourselves, so He accepted your repentance and forgave you. So now, have relations with them and seek that which Allah has decreed for you. And eat and drink until the white thread of dawn becomes distinct to you from the black thread [of night]. Then complete the fast until the sunset. And do not have relations with them as long as you are staying for worship in the mosques. These are the limits [set by] Allah, so do not approach them. Thus does Allah make clear His ordinances to the people that they may become righteous.

78. O you who have believed, what is [the matter] with you that, when you are told to go forth in the cause of Allah, you adhere heavily to the earth? Are you satisfied with the life of this world rather than the Hereafter? But what is the enjoyment of worldly life compared to the Hereafter except a [very] little. If you do not go forth, He will punish you with a painful punishment and will replace you with another people, and you will not harm Him at all. And Allah is over all things competent. If you do not aid the Prophet—Allah has already aided him when those who disbelieved had driven him out [of Makkah] as one of two, when they were in the cave and he said to his companion, "Do not grieve; indeed Allah is with us." And Allah sent down his tranquillity upon him and supported him with angels you did not see and made the word of those who disbelieved the lowest, while the word of Allah—that is the highest. And Allah is Exalted in Might and Wise.

One should remember that one of the purpose and goal of a Muslim is to make dawah on the path of Allah ﷻ as mentioned إِذَا قِيلَ لَكُمُ انفِرُواْ فِي سَبِيلِ اللَّهِ. This is the unique feature of this ummah that actually differentiates and elevates us compares to other ummahs. This is mentioned in كُنتُمْ[79]

خَيْرَ أُمَّةٍ أُخْرِجَتْ لِلنَّاسِ تَأْمُرُونَ بِالْمَعْرُوفِ وَتَنْهَوْنَ عَنِ الْمُنكَرِ وَتُؤْمِنُونَ بِاللَّهِ وَلَوْ آمَنَ أَهْلُ الْكِتَابِ لَكَانَ خَيْرًا لَّهُم مِّنْهُمُ الْمُؤْمِنُونَ وَأَكْثَرُهُمُ الْفَاسِقُونَ {آل عمران/110}

Yet, in this assigned and noble responsibility of tabligh, nahy-I anil munkar and amr bil ma'ruf, sometimes the person can feel that he or she is alone in the game. No one is helping him or her.

At these times, it is important that the person should remember that Allah ﷻ is sufficient for the person as mentioned in the above ayah as لَا تَحْزَنْ إِنَّ اللَّهَ مَعَنَا.

Nifāq, Dispute and Possible Chaos in the Works of the Deen

One should remember that Allah ﷻ is the one who gives harmony, the same purpose or goal to work on the same purpose to achieve a common goal. It is not due to a charismatic leader or benefits received by being part of the group. Allah ﷻ is the One Who sets the hearts for the same direction and goal as mentioned [80]

وَإِن يُرِيدُواْ أَن يَخْدَعُوكَ فَإِنَّ حَسْبَكَ اللَّهُ هُوَ الَّذِيَ أَيَّدَكَ بِنَصْرِهِ وَبِالْمُؤْمِنِينَ {الأنفال/62}
وَأَلَّفَ بَيْنَ قُلُوبِهِمْ لَوْ أَنفَقْتَ مَا فِي الأَرْضِ جَمِيعاً مَّا أَلَّفَتَ بَيْنَ قُلُوبِهِمْ وَلَكِنَّ اللَّهَ أَلَّفَ بَيْنَهُمْ إِنَّهُ عَزِيزٌ حَكِيمٌ {الأنفال/63} يَا أَيُّهَا النَّبِيُّ حَسْبُكَ اللَّهُ وَمَنِ اتَّبَعَكَ مِنَ الْمُؤْمِنِينَ {الأنفال/64} يَا أَيُّهَا النَّبِيُّ حَرِّضِ الْمُؤْمِنِينَ عَلَى الْقِتَالِ إِن يَكُن مِّنكُمْ عِشْرُونَ صَابِرُونَ يَغْلِبُواْ مِئَتَيْنِ وَإِن يَكُن مِّنكُم مِّئَةٌ يَغْلِبُواْ أَلْفًا مِّنَ الَّذِينَ كَفَرُواْ بِأَنَّهُمْ قَوْمٌ لاَّ يَفْقَهُونَ {الأنفال/65}

---

79. You are the best nation produced [as an example] for mankind. You enjoin what is right and forbid what is wrong and believe in Allah. If only the People of the Scripture had believed, it would have been better for them. Among them are believers, but most of them are defiantly disobedient.

80. But if they intend to deceive you—then sufficient for you is Allah. It is He who supported you with His help and with the believers And brought together their hearts. If you had spent all that is in the earth, you could not have brought their hearts together; but Allah brought them together. Indeed, He is Exalted in Might and Wise. O Prophet, sufficient for you is Allah and for whoever follows you of the believers. O Prophet, urge the believers to battle. If there are among you twenty [who are] steadfast, they will overcome two hundred. And if there are among you one hundred [who are] steadfast, they will overcome a thousand of those who have disbelieved because they are a people who do not understand.

One should remember that Allah ☀ is the One who protects the person and group of people from the nifāq and plot of others as mentioned وَإِن يُرِيدُواْ أَن يَخْدَعُوكَ فَإِنَّ حَسْبَكَ اللَّهُ

One should remember that Allah ☀ is the One who unites the people's hearts for the same noble and high goal and purpose as mentioned وَلَٰكِنَّ أَلَّفَ بَيْنَهُمْ اللَّهُ.

One should remember that Allah ☀ alone is sufficient for the person and group of believers in spite of their small numbers to be on the works of the deen as mentioned يَا أَيُّهَا النَّبِيُّ حَسْبُكَ اللَّهُ وَمَنِ اتَّبَعَكَ مِنَ الْمُؤْمِنِينَ [81] {الأنفال/64}

One should remember that the true position of a Muslim requires to be in the works of the Deen and encourage people for this goal as mentioned يَا أَيُّهَا النَّبِيُّ حَرِّضِ الْمُؤْمِنِينَ.

Loss of Ni'mahs

ذَٰلِكَ بِأَنَّ اللَّهَ لَمْ يَكُ مُغَيِّرًا نِّعْمَةً أَنْعَمَهَا عَلَىٰ قَوْمٍ حَتَّىٰ يُغَيِّرُواْ مَا بِأَنفُسِهِمْ وَأَنَّ اللَّهَ سَمِيعٌ عَلِيمٌ [82] {الأنفال/53}

لَهُ مُعَقِّبَاتٌ مِّن بَيْنِ يَدَيْهِ وَمِنْ خَلْفِهِ يَحْفَظُونَهُ مِنْ أَمْرِ اللَّهِ إِنَّ اللَّهَ لاَ يُغَيِّرُ مَا بِقَوْمٍ حَتَّىٰ يُغَيِّرُواْ مَا بِأَنْفُسِهِمْ وَإِذَا أَرَادَ اللَّهُ بِقَوْمٍ سُوءًا فَلاَ مَرَدَّ لَهُ وَمَا لَهُم مِّن دُونِهِ مِن وَالٍ {الرعد/11}

One should remember that Allah ☀ keeps the person or group of people on guidance and bestowing different openings on this path to them as long as the person and this group tries to follow the path with the guidelines of the Qurān and sunnah of Rasulullah ☀. In the externalities of this path of the person or this group, the external guidelines should fit and be in the line of the Qurān and Sunnah of Rasulullah ☀.

In its internalities, the person or the group should maintain the ikhlas for the sake of Allah ☀ far from group or personal identities of arrogance, wealth, knowledge position or title related struggles of hasad, jealousy and motivational problems of riya, showing off.

---

81. O Prophet, sufficient for you is Allah and for whoever follows you of the believers.
82. That is because Allah would not change a favor which He had bestowed upon a people until they change what is within themselves. And indeed, Allah is Hearing and Knowing. For each one are successive [angels] before and behind him who protect him by the decree of Allah. Indeed, Allah will not change the condition of a people until they change what is in themselves. And when Allah intends for a people ill, there is no repelling it. And there is not for them besides Him any patron.

There can be a positive group identity with the guidelines of sunnah and the Qurãn. Yet, this positive group or personal identity should embody inclusiveness. This identity should not display the features of exclusiveness leading to arrogance. It should have the non-judgmental approaches of tasawwuf that any person can be from ahlulullah so one should not break one's heart implicitly or explicitly by involving themselves with the arrogant traps of identities.

There can be a positive disposition of having gibta for the ones who have worldly titles while engaging with the works of the deen. This gibta as a positive disposition can make the person desire to have the similar means such as wealth or knowledge in order to use these means effectively for the sake of Allah ﷻ. Yet, one cannot desire the loss of this ni'mah on their brother or sister. If one desires even a little bit loss of this ni'mah of Allah ﷻ on their brother or sister, then this person indeed engages oneself with hasad which can destroy the person himself or herself.

There can be a positive disposition of encouraging people to do the khayr-good by showing some role models, and by implementing best practice sharing. Yet, this should not be the essence of one's or group's motivation that can lead to riya-show off. The example of riya-show off can display itself by doing something in order to be a role model or example for others but not for the pleasure of Allah ﷻ. Yet, everything in their essence should be performed to please Allah ﷻ.

Moving Forward with Ikhlas

With these possibilities, if a person or a group includes some of these diseases in their engagement of dawah or works of deens as mentioned above, then it is possible that Allah ﷻ can replace these people or individuals with others who can work, give and take for the sake of Allah ﷻ as mentioned [83] {محمد/38} وَإِن تَتَوَلَّوْا يَسْتَبْدِلْ قَوْمًا غَيْرَكُمْ ثُمَّ لَا يَكُونُوا أَمْثَالَكُم. Yet, there is always the possibility of making tawbah to Allah ﷻ in all the problematic engagements. Allah ﷻ is al-Gafûr and al-Rahìm.

---

83. Here you are—those invited to spend in the cause of Allah—but among you are those who withhold [out of greed]. And whoever withholds only withholds [benefit] from himself; and Allah is the Free of need, while you are the needy. And if you turn away, He will replace you with another people; then they will not be the likes of you.

Yet, one should remember that the people who have ikhlas regardless of their small numbers should continue to work on the path of Allah ﷻ with ikhlas without being discouraged due to to disputes or chaos among their past or present associates. Allah ﷻ can empower the people who continue to struggle on the Divine path as the real purpose of existence.

Regardless of their number, weakness and chaotic disposition of the past or present members, Allah ﷻ can give barakah in the engagements of the ones who have ikhlas to please Allah ﷻ. This is mentioned as: [84]

يَا أَيُّهَا النَّبِيُّ حَسْبُكَ اللّهُ وَمَنِ اتَّبَعَكَ مِنَ الْمُؤْمِنِينَ {الأنفال/64} يَا أَيُّهَا النَّبِيُّ حَرِّضِ الْمُؤْمِنِينَ عَلَى الْقِتَالِ إِن يَكُن مِّنكُمْ عِشْرُونَ صَابِرُونَ يَغْلِبُواْ مِئَتَيْنِ وَإِن يَكُن مِّنكُم مِّئَةٌ يَغْلِبُواْ أَلْفًا مِّنَ الَّذِينَ كَفَرُواْ بِأَنَّهُمْ قَوْمٌ لاَّ يَفْقَهُونَ {الأنفال/65}

إِلاَّ تَنصُرُوهُ فَقَدْ نَصَرَهُ اللّهُ إِذْ أَخْرَجَهُ الَّذِينَ كَفَرُواْ ثَانِيَ اثْنَيْنِ إِذْ هُمَا فِي الْغَارِ إِذْ يَقُولُ لِصَاحِبِهِ لاَ تَحْزَنْ إِنَّ اللّهَ مَعَنَا فَأَنزَلَ اللّهُ سَكِينَتَهُ عَلَيْهِ وَأَيَّدَهُ بِجُنُودٍ لَّمْ تَرَوْهَا وَجَعَلَ كَلِمَةَ الَّذِينَ كَفَرُواْ السُّفْلَى وَكَلِمَةُ اللّهِ هِيَ الْعُلْيَا وَاللّهُ عَزِيزٌ حَكِيمٌ {التوبة/40}

Juz 12

Sûrah 12 – Yûsuf

Tazkiya: Struggles of Balancing the Tendencies & Spiritual Frictions

وَلَقَدْ هَمَّتْ بِهِ وَهَمَّ بِهَا لَوْلا أَن رَّأَى بُرْهَانَ رَبِّهِ كَذَلِكَ لِنَصْرِفَ عَنْهُ السُّوءَ وَالْفَحْشَاء إِنَّهُ مِنْ عِبَادِنَا الْمُخْلَصِينَ [85] {يوسف/24}

---

84. O Prophet, sufficient for you is Allah and for whoever follows you of the believers. O Prophet, urge the believers to battle. If there are among you twenty [who are] steadfast, they will overcome two hundred. And if there are among you one hundred [who are] steadfast, they will overcome a thousand of those who have If you do not aid the Prophet—Allah has already aided him when those who disbelieved had driven him out [of Makkah] as one of two, when they were in the cave and he said to his companion, "Do not grieve; indeed Allah is with us." And Allah sent down his tranquillity upon him and supported him with angels you did not see and made the word of those who disbelieved the lowest, while the word of Allah—that is the highest. And Allah is Exalted in Might and Wise.
85. And she certainly determined [to seduce] him, and he would have inclined to her had he not seen the proof of his Lord. And thus [it was] that We should avert from him evil and immorality. Indeed, he was of Our chosen servants.

As humans we have tendencies. A man has a tendency for the opposite gender. A woman can have a tendency for the opposite gender. If there is no tendency, then this can be considered as abnormality. These tendencies can be indicated in وَلَقَدْ هَمَّتْ بِهِ وَهَمَّ بِهَا.

Yet, these tendencies should be guided with the guidelines of halāl and harām as designated by Allah ﷻ with the teachings of the Qurān and Sunnah of Rasulullah ﷺ. The relationships within the marriage is halāl and encouraged as mentioned by Rasulullah ﷺ as sadaqah [7] (hadith # 1674). The relationships outside marriage is haram and disliked and unapproved by Allah ﷻ in these guidelines. May Allah ﷻ protect us.

Beyond these clear guidelines of halal and haram relationships, most of us face in practical life the gray or intermediate areas of these boundaries becoming convoluted and complicated. This is not only related with gender relationships but other guidelines of halal or haram as outlined by Allah ﷻ and Rasulullah ﷺ. For example, a person knows that hasad or thinking bad (su-I zan) or talking bad others is haram. Yet, the person can still engage with oneself in a self dialogue of hasad for another person, and yet, Allah ﷻ knows all of them.

At this point of self-dialogue, the struggles of the person against this trial or test can reveal the real internal position of the person. The choice is always whether he or she executes these possibilities within the struggles of the self in a way that Allah ﷻ is pleased with the person or not.

Even, if take this case وَلَقَدْ هَمَّتْ بِهِ وَهَمَّ بِهَا, Allah ﷻ mentions this self-incited natural phenomenon when two opposite genders are in the same closed room. Yet, at this position, the person cannot and should not engage with the arrogant deceptive dialogues of piety such as "I don't have any interest in the opposite gender. I can control myself. My will power is at such a level that I don't engage in haram." These are all wrong and very dangerous dispositions which can possibly attract the makr of Allah ﷻ, trials and tests to prove the person the reality.

In all dispositions and in this disposition, the person is expected to refuge in Allah ﷻ with weakness, ajz, faqr, spiritual poverty and at the same time, with an inner struggle of executing the logic and reason over the emotions with the struggles of verbalizing and even imitating the halal. Or, in some cases, one can isolate oneself from the haram even his or her emotions can overwhelmingly can shout and insist for otherwise or for opposite inclination dragging the person into destruction.

Yes, sometimes it is very difficult to control one's emotions stemming from anger, hasad, lust, seeking position or recognition or wealth. Yet, in all these dispositions one should still try to unshackle oneself from the chains of these powerful emotions and incline towards the high values as set by Allah ☙ in the Qurān and through the teachings of Rasulullah ﷺ.

This is extremely difficult. Yet, this is the real struggle.

Most of the struggle or battle occurs in these areas that the person knows the problem and he or she has the choice to proceed or not to please or displease Allah ☙.

Pushing oneself to do the right choice as an imitation even at times can be very critical. Yet, this should be fused with the the immediate and synchronized rush of taking refuge in Allah ☙.

One should remember that our internal spiritual equipment have friction and inertia. The friction is a force acting against direction of the motion. Our struggles are the motion. The natural existent force is the friction of anger, hasad, lust and other diseases that need to be overcome with a threshold energy.

Yet, in physics, there is a healthy friction that keeps and prevents things from falling apart and making them stay still in sakina. Similarly, the healty anger, hasad as gibta, or healthy lust in one's relationship with their spouse or the desire to eat food in order not to die are all healthy frictions that can deep the person's spiritual faculties into the oceans of sakina.

The Source of all sakina is from Allah ☙ as mentioned اللهم انت السلام و منك السلام[1]. In fact, Allah ☙ is as-Salām. Therefore, when one constantly rushes to Allah ☙ then, the person dives into the infinite ocean of sakina.

Yet, in all these struggles, there is one condition of achievement. That is not depending oneself, but depending on Allah ☙. Constantly running to Allah ☙ with firar, constantly turning to Allah ☙ with tawbah, constantly going back to Allah ☙ with awbah and inabah are the key elements to embody faqr and ajz, the spiritual poverty and weakness in front of Rabbul Alamin, As-Samad.

Therefore, we constantly remember this required disposition in Sûrah Fatiha as [86] {الفاتحة/5} إِيَّاكَ نَعْبُدُ وإِيَّاكَ نَسْتَعِينُ with the repetition of إِيَّاكَ. This builds ihlas and sincerity in the person as mukhlas.

---

86. It is You we worship and You we ask for help.

In all these cases, Allah ﷻ always but always help as mentioned لَوْلَا أَن رَّأَى بُرْهَانَ رَبِّهِ كَذَلِكَ لِنَصْرِفَ عَنْهُ السُّوءَ وَالْفَحْشَاء. Allah ﷻ always help the ones who are muhlas إِنَّهُ مِنْ عِبَادِنَا الْمُخْلَصِينَ {24/يوسف} [87]

This process of constant going to Allah ﷻ as tawbah, inabah, awbah instilling ikhlas in the person can be called tazkiya which can be defined as the struggle of the nafs or ego in these frictions of spiritual diseases with the help, I'ana of Allah ﷻ as the person only goes back to Allah ﷻ in external forms referred as 'I'badah.

Yes, one cannot really systemize going back to Allah ﷻ unless it is through 'ibadah. The highest level of this systemization is through the required prayers, fardh. Fardh prayers include fully all the tawbah, inabah, awbah, firār and taking refuge in Allah ﷻ. Then, the person is washed in the river of sakinah five times a day as mentioned by Rasulullah 1] ﷺ].

When the person embodies this attitude inshAllah, the true tazkiya comes only with the Fadl and Rahmah of Allah ﷻ as mentioned [88] وَلَوْلَا فَضْلُ اللَّهِ عَلَيْكُمْ وَرَحْمَتُهُ مَا زَكَا مِنكُم مِّنْ أَحَدٍ أَبَدًا وَلَكِنَّ اللَّهَ يُزَكِّي مَن يَشَاء وَاللَّهُ سَمِيعٌ عَلِيمٌ {21/النور}

Juz 15

Sûrah 17 al-Isrã

[12]

Detailing of the Qurãn about Nature in Teaching Marifatullah

وَجَعَلْنَا اللَّيْلَ وَالنَّهَارَ آيَتَيْنِ فَمَحَوْنَا آيَةَ اللَّيْلِ وَجَعَلْنَا آيَةَ النَّهَارِ مُبْصِرَةً لِتَبْتَغُواْ فَضْلاً مِّن رَّبِّكُمْ وَلِتَعْلَمُواْ عَدَدَ السِّنِينَ وَالْحِسَابَ وَكُلَّ شَيْءٍ فَصَّلْنَاهُ تَفْصِيلاً [89] {12/الإسراء}

---

87. And she certainly determined [to seduce] him, and he would have inclined to her had he not seen the proof of his Lord. And thus [it was] that We should avert from him evil and immorality. Indeed, he was of Our chosen servants.

88. O you who have believed, do not follow the footsteps of Satan. And whoever follows the footsteps of Satan—indeed, he enjoins immorality and wrongdoing. And if not for the favor of Allah upon you and His mercy, not one of you would have been pure, ever, but Allah purifies whom He wills, and Allah is Hearing and Knowing.

89. And We have made the night and day two signs, and We erased the sign of the night and made the sign of the day visible that you may seek bounty from your Lord and may know the number of years and the account [of time]. And everything We have set out in detail.

It is important to understand that the Qurān explains the realities related with the imān and marifutullah in detail. At another perspective, Allah ﷻ makes science and scientific explanations in the nature available in detail in order people to reach knowledge about imān and its realities with marifatullah.

Our free will with free choice indicates and leads to using our inclinations to convince our own selves. This is a lifelong struggle. It does not and may not happen often immediately.

If Allah ﷻ wished, a sign or ayah can have made all humans to fully submit to Allah ﷻ as mentioned [90] إِن نَّشَأْ نُنَزِّلْ عَلَيْهِم مِّن السَّمَاء آيَةً فَظَلَّتْ أَعْنَاقُهُمْ لَهَا خَاضِعِينَ {الشعراء/4}.

Yet, this is not the purpose and goal.

Adab of Learning

In this regard, a good teacher can explain in detail the questions.

Yet, adab of learning and questioning is always related with the people's intention in learning. In other words, questioning for the sake of challenging or arrogance is an attitude without adab.

Although it is difficult to maintain the composure at these times if someone is teaching, yet one should still not assume but do their most effort to teach without any judgment especially at our times of Western dominance where constant questioning is promoted and encouraged as a norm.

It is important to teach the manners of adab to Muslim children in learning, questioning, and other etiquettes in interaction as our pious salaf implemented and embodied as inspired by the Qurān and Sunnah of Rasulullah ﷺ.

Learning without adab can generate people and youth pumped up with fake arrogance far from our values of adab. The individualistic societies in the West is the natural outcome of this pseudo-inspired self-sufficient individuals with confidence.

Learning with adab can generate people and youth that can plant seeds of generations and youth who themselves can maintain inner peace with their own selves and others. The social life in Eastern

---

90. If We willed, We could send down to them from the sky a sign for which their necks would remain humbled.

cultures besides many of their problems is still the nature outcome of this remnant teachings of adab in these societies.

[85]

Primary Life: Soul-Rûh

وَيَسْأَلُونَكَ عَنِ الرُّوحِ قُلِ الرُّوحُ مِنْ أَمْرِ رَبِّي وَمَا أُوتِيتُم مِّن الْعِلْمِ إِلاَّ قَلِيلاً ⁹¹
{الإسراء/85}

When we review the ayahs of the Qurān about the rûh, الرُّوح translated as soul in Enlish, one can find different perspectives although its knowledge may be limited as mentioned in this ayah.

In its primary meaning, one can find the meaning of the life that is given to us initially by Allah ﷻ as mentioned with ⁹² مِن فِيهِ وَنَفَخَ سَوَّاهُ ثُمَّ رُوحِهِ. وَجَعَلَ لَكُمُ السَّمْعَ وَالْأَبْصَارَ وَالْأَفْئِدَةَ قَلِيلًا مَّا تَشْكُرُونَ {السجدة/9}. In this ayah, life mentioned with وَنَفَخَ فِيهِ مِن رُّوحِهِ can be the primary realization of the person's being with his or her life as given and bestowed by Allah ﷻ.

The bodily engagements such as the organs, eyes or hearing as mentioned in وَجَعَلَ لَكُمُ السَّمْعَ وَالْأَبْصَارَ وَالْأَفْئِدَةَ are all dependent on existence but not primary. There is no meaning of a body without life even though the body may be still intact with all its organs such as the eyes or ear.

In this context, one can consider and remember the funeral scenes of a full intact corpse of human body without life. Although there is the full body, people rush to "get rid of it" meaning that they don't believe that this body has the same full features of a living human. Therefore, this body should no longer belong to the social life of living humans although a few minutes ago or hours ago, this body was talking to them before its dead.

All these discussions prove that the primary and essence what we call or define as "humans" is the thing that gives life to it. This thing in terminology as referred in the Qurān is rûh, الرُّوحُ and translated as soul in English.

---

91. Say, "Each works according to his manner, but your Lord is most knowing of who is best guided in way."

92. Then He proportioned him and breathed into him from His [created] soul and made for you hearing and vision and hearts; little are you grateful.

Self-Nafs: Tool of Realization

After this primary self-realization of existence referred as rûh as existent given primarily condition of being a human, then the body can be considered to serve as a tool or vehicle.

At another note, one call this self-realization as nafs or self. Self or Nafs is expected to realize their own existence and their own life referred as rûh.

In this regard, all the beings that we see and realize in the universe as animals, plants, animated or animated beings are in full realization of their existence. Therefore, they make shukr, show gratitude, and appreciation to Allah ﷻ in different forms of dhikr. One can remember the ayahs of the Qurān as [93] أَلَمْ تَرَ أَنَّ اللَّهَ يُسَبِّحُ لَهُ مَن فِي السَّمَاوَاتِ وَالْأَرْضِ وَالطَّيْرُ صَافَّاتٍ كُلٌّ قَدْ عَلِمَ صَلَاتَهُ وَتَسْبِيحَهُ وَاللَّهُ عَلِيمٌ بِمَا يَفْعَلُونَ {النور/41}

ثُمَّ قَسَتْ قُلُوبُكُم مِّن بَعْدِ ذَٰلِكَ فَهِيَ كَالْحِجَارَةِ أَوْ أَشَدُّ قَسْوَةً وَإِنَّ مِنَ الْحِجَارَةِ لَمَا يَتَفَجَّرُ مِنْهُ الْأَنْهَارُ وَإِنَّ مِنْهَا لَمَا يَشَّقَّقُ فَيَخْرُجُ مِنْهُ الْمَاء وَإِنَّ مِنْهَا لَمَا يَهْبِطُ مِنْ خَشْيَةِ اللَّهِ وَمَا اللَّهُ بِغَافِلٍ عَمَّا تَعْمَلُونَ {البقرة/74}

لَوْ أَنزَلْنَا هَٰذَا الْقُرْآنَ عَلَى جَبَلٍ لَّرَأَيْتَهُ خَاشِعًا مُّتَصَدِّعًا مِّنْ خَشْيَةِ اللَّهِ وَتِلْكَ الْأَمْثَالُ نَضْرِبُهَا لِلنَّاسِ لَعَلَّهُمْ يَتَفَكَّرُونَ {الحشر/21}

At this point, what differentiates humans and Jinn from everything is their additional given tool. This is called free will, taklîf, masûliyah and free decision making. One can review the ayahs

---

93. Do you not see that Allah is exalted by whomever is within the heavens and the earth and [by] the birds with wings spread [in flight]? Each [of them] has known his [means of] prayer and exalting [Him], and Allah is Knowing of what they do. Then your hearts became hardened after that, being like stones or even harder. For indeed, there are stones from which rivers burst forth, and there are some of them that split open and water comes out, and there are some of them that fall down for fear of Allah. And Allah is not unaware of what you do. If We had sent down this Qurán upon a mountain, you would have seen it humbled and coming apart from fear of Allah. And these examples We present to the people that perhaps they will give thought.

As ٩٤ إِنَّا عَرَضْنَا الْأَمَانَةَ عَلَى السَّمَاوَاتِ وَالْأَرْضِ وَالْجِبَالِ فَأَبَيْنَ أَن يَحْمِلْنَهَا وَأَشْفَقْنَ
مِنْهَا وَحَمَلَهَا الْإِنسَانُ إِنَّهُ كَانَ ظَلُومًا جَهُولًا {الأحزاب/72}

لَا إِكْرَاهَ فِي الدِّينِ قَد تَّبَيَّنَ الرُّشْدُ مِنَ الْغَيِّ فَمَن يَكْفُرْ بِالطَّاغُوتِ وَيُؤْمِن بِاللَّهِ فَقَدِ اسْتَمْسَكَ
بِالْعُرْوَةِ الْوُثْقَىٰ لَا انفِصَامَ لَهَا وَاللَّهُ سَمِيعٌ عَلِيمٌ {البقرة/256}

Yet, this additional bonus "million dollar" or "fortune" can make a lot of humans and Jinn arrogant and heedless due to their additional fortune or wealth. Then, the person can choose to follow the path of kufr. Due to arrogance, he or she may get so pumped up to claim their own deity like the Firawn explicitly from humans in front of the Prophet of Allah ﷺ, Musa as showing him all the miracles as mentioned ٩٥ فَقَالَ أَنَا رَبُّكُمُ الْأَعْلَى {النازعات/24}.

Or he or she may get so pumped up to claim their own identity implicitly from Jinn like the Shaytān in the presence of Rabbul Alamìn and say ٩٦ قَالَ أَنَا خَيْرٌ مِّنْهُ خَلَقْتَنِي مِن نَّارٍ وَخَلَقْتَهُ مِن طِينٍ {ص/٧٦}. In this sense, these humans and Jinn go to the lowest of low in ranking among all beings such as animals, animated or unanimated beings.

On the other hand, this additional bonus "million dollar" or "fortune" can make some maybe few humans and Jinn, realize this fortune bestowed by Allah ﷺ with their own self-realization and existence. This realization can lead them to humbleness and humility of tawhid, Islam and imān. Due to this humbleness and humility towards all the bounties of Allah ﷺ, then they try to embody this gratitude to Allah ﷺ. This embodiment of gratitude can be called being "'abd" of Allah ﷺ. In this position of the self realization or nafs, the person now tries to actualize this u'budiyyah to Allah ﷺ with their free will and free choice with the Fadl and Rahmah of Allah ﷺ. In this regard, one can see the epitome of 'ibadah as Rasulullah ﷺ who even surpassed all the beings including the angels in his ﷺ level before Rabbul Alamìn, Allah

---

94. Indeed, we offered the Trust to the heavens and the earth and the mountains, and they declined to bear it and feared it; but man [undertook to] bear it. Indeed, he was unjust and ignorant. There shall be no compulsion in [acceptance of] the religion. The right course has become clear from the wrong. So whoever disbelieves in Taghut and believes in Allah has grasped the most trustworthy handhold with no break in it. And Allah is Hearing and Knowing.
95. And said, "I am your most exalted lord."
96. He said, "I am better than him. You created me from fire and created him from clay."

سُبْحَانَ الَّذِي أَسْرَى بِعَبْدِهِ لَيْلًا مِّنَ الْمَسْجِدِ الْحَرَامِ إِلَى الْمَسْجِدِ الْأَقْصَى ﷽ as mentioned ⁹⁷
الَّذِي بَارَكْنَا حَوْلَهُ لِنُرِيَهُ مِنْ آيَاتِنَا إِنَّهُ هُوَ السَّمِيعُ البَصِيرُ {الإسراء/1}

One should realize that with this primary condition of life or existence referred as rûh-soul, then nafs-self is the realization of this life and existence.

Secondary Life with Wahiy

With the Fadl and Rahmah of Allah ﷻ, Allah ﷻ bestowed on us the wahiy, the Divine Guidance through the scriptures and prophets in order to help us as to truly realize the existence of their own life and existence but not side tracked with the additional "million dollar" bonus given to humans referred as free will, or free choice with the pumps of arrogance or false self identity claims.

In this regard, all the scriptures and prophets sent by Allah ﷻ are another form of life that makes us truly realize the real meaning of our life and the purpose of existence.

Today, the Qurān and Sunnah of Rasulullah ﷺ is the life to revive the dead and sick souls and give them the true meaning of their own meaning, purpose, existence and life.

One can review the ayahs clearly indicating this position as: ⁹⁸

وَكَذَلِكَ أَوْحَيْنَا إِلَيْكَ رُوحًا مِّنْ أَمْرِنَا مَا كُنتَ تَدْرِي مَا الْكِتَابُ وَلَا الْإِيمَانُ وَلَكِن جَعَلْنَاهُ
نُورًا نَّهْدِي بِهِ مَنْ نَّشَاء مِنْ عِبَادِنَا وَإِنَّكَ لَتَهْدِي إِلَى صِرَاطٍ مُسْتَقِيم {الشورى/52}

لَا تَجِدُ قَوْمًا يُؤْمِنُونَ بِاللَّهِ وَالْيَوْمِ الْآخِرِ يُوَادُّونَ مَنْ حَادَّ اللَّهَ وَرَسُولَهُ وَلَوْ كَانُوا آبَاءهُمْ
أَوْ أَبْنَاءهُمْ أَوْ إِخْوَانَهُمْ أَوْ عَشِيرَتَهُمْ أُوْلَئِكَ كَتَبَ فِي قُلُوبِهِمُ الْإِيمَانَ وَأَيَّدَهُم بِرُوحٍ مِّنْهُ
وَيُدْخِلُهُمْ جَنَّاتٍ تَجْرِي مِن تَحْتِهَا الْأَنْهَارُ خَالِدِينَ فِيهَا رَضِيَ اللَّهُ عَنْهُمْ وَرَضُواْ عَنْهُ
أُوْلَئِكَ حِزْبُ اللَّهِ أَلَا إِنَّ حِزْبَ اللَّهِ هُمُ الْمُفْلِحُونَ ⁹⁹ {المجادلة/22}

---

97. Exalted is He who took His Servant by night from al-Masjid al-Haram to al-Masjid al-Aqsa, whose surroundings We have blessed, to show him of Our signs. Indeed, He is the Hearing, the Seeing.
98. And thus We have revealed to you an inspiration of Our command. You did not know what is the Book or [what is] faith, but We have made it a light by which We guide whom We will of Our servants. And indeed, [O Muhammad], you guide to a straight path
99. You will not find a people who believe in Allah and the Last Day having affection for those who oppose Allah and His Messenger, even if they were their fathers or their sons or their brothers or their kindred. Those—He has decreed within their hearts faith and supported them with spirit from Him. And We will admit them to gardens beneath which rivers flow, wherein they abide eternally. Allah is pleased with them, and they are pleased with Him— those are the party of Allah. Unquestionably, the party of Allah—they are the successful.

Ruhul Quddus and Isa as

One can now understand the technical term as "Ruhul Quddus" as given to the title of Jibril as interpreted by the muffassirûn. Jibril as has brought the wahiy to all the prophets (as). In this sense, wahiy is the life given to humans by Allah ﷻ as delivered by Jibril as.

In this sense, engaging with the shi'ar of Allah ﷻ such as the Qurãn as the source of life, Jibril as the Blessed and Noble Deliverer of the life of wahiy and all the prophets of Allah ﷻ as the receiver of the life of wahiy can also give life to us.

Yet, Christians fall in to the mistake of distancing themselves from tawhid with trinity in their misunderstanding of Ruhul Qudus as the Deliverer of the Life and receiver of this life from Ruhul Qudus. Ruhul Qudus as Jibril as is similar to other angels in his position with Rabbul Alamìn as mentioned [100] تَعْرُجُ الْمَلَائِكَةُ وَالرُّوحُ إِلَيْهِ فِي يَوْمٍ كَانَ مِقْدَارُهُ خَمْسِينَ أَلْفَ سَنَةٍ {المعارج/4}

يَوْمَ يَقُومُ الرُّوحُ وَالْمَلَائِكَةُ صَفًّا لَّا يَتَكَلَّمُونَ إِلَّا مَنْ أَذِنَ لَهُ الرحمَنُ وَقَالَ صَوَابًا {النبأ/38}

تَنَزَّلُ الْمَلَائِكَةُ وَالرُّوحُ فِيهَا بِإِذْنِ رَبِّهِم مِّن كُلِّ أَمْرٍ {القدر/4}

فَاتَّخَذَتْ مِن دُونِهِمْ حِجَابًا فَأَرْسَلْنَا إِلَيْهَا رُوحَنَا فَتَمَثَّلَ لَهَا بَشَرًا سَوِيًّا {مريم/17} [101] قَالَتْ إِنِّي أَعُوذُ بِالرَّحْمَنِ مِنكَ إِن كُنتَ تَقِيًّا {مريم/18} قَالَ إِنَّمَا أَنَا رَسُولُ رَبِّكِ لِأَهَبَ لَكِ غُلَامًا زَكِيًّا {مريم/19}

They forget the sunnatullah that whoever engages with the shi'ar of these sources of life, they can get some type of life in different quantities and qualities. Even, this engagement is done with wrong intentions. Yet they may still receive the effect of life of them as mentioned [102] قَالَ بَصُرْتُ بِمَا لَمْ يَبْصُرُوا بِهِ فَقَبَضْتُ قَبْضَةً مِّنْ أَثَرِ الرَّسُولِ فَنَبَذْتُهَا وَكَذَلِكَ سَوَّلَتْ لِي نَفْسِي {طه/96}

---

100. The angels and the Spirit will ascend to Him during a Day the extent of which is fifty thousand years. The Day that the Spirit and the angels will stand in rows, they will not speak except for one whom the Most Merciful permits, and he will say what is correct. The angels and the Spirit descend therein by permission of their Lord for every matter.
101. And she took, in seclusion from them, a screen. Then We sent to her Our Angel, and he represented himself She said, "Indeed, I seek refuge in the Most Merciful from you, [so leave me], if you should be fearing of Allah." He said, "I am only the messenger of your Lord to give you [news of] a pure boy."
102. He said, "I am only the messenger of your Lord to give you [news of] a pure boy."

According to the mufassirûn, مِّنْ أَثَرِ الرَّسُولِ are the traces of Jibril as, Ruhul Qudus. Samiri took some traces after he left and tried to give life to a calf. Then, calf showed some type of life symtomps. SubhanAllah! even, the traces of shiar of the Blessed Delivery of Life, Jibril as as the Ruhul Quddus can have an effect.

Yet, people, in this case Christians, forget and make the big and huge mistake of mixing the projection or reflection with the essence. Allah ﷻ is the Only, One, True, Absolute Source of Life as Al-Hayy and Al-Qayyum as mentioned [103] فَإِذَا سَوَّيْتُهُ وَنَفَخْتُ فِيهِ مِن رُّوحِي فَقَعُوا لَهُ سَاجِدِينَ {ص/72}.

رَفِيعُ الدَّرَجَاتِ ذُو الْعَرْشِ يُلْقِي الرُّوحَ مِنْ أَمْرِهِ عَلَى مَن يَشَاء مِنْ عِبَادِهِ لِيُنذِرَ يَوْمَ التَّلَاقِ {غافر/15}

Ruhul Qudus and all the prophets including Isa as are the blessed and noble shi'ar of delivery of this life from Allah ﷻ.

In this sense, Isa as also has the direct relation of the Deliverer of the Life, Jibril as, Ruhul Qudus through his mother as mentioned [104] فَاتَّخَذَتْ مِن دُونِهِمْ حِجَابًا فَأَرْسَلْنَا إِلَيْهَا رُوحَنَا فَتَمَثَّلَ لَهَا بَشَرًا سَوِيًّا {مريم/17} قَالَتْ إِنِّي أَعُوذُ بِالرَّحْمَن مِنكَ إِن كُنتَ تَقِيًّا {مريم/18} قَالَ إِنَّمَا أَنَا رَسُولُ رَبِّكِ لِأَهَبَ لَكِ غُلَامًا زَكِيًّا {مريم/19}

Therefore, due to this special position of being in the effect of Ruhul Qudus, Jibril as, he can have similar traces of life with the permission and enablement of Allah ﷻ as mentioned [105] إِذْ قَالَ اللّهُ يَا عِيسى ابْنَ مَرْيَمَ اذْكُرْ نِعْمَتِي عَلَيْكَ وَعَلَى وَالِدَتِكَ إِذْ أَيَّدتُّكَ بِرُوحِ الْقُدُسِ تُكَلِّمُ النَّاسَ فِي الْمَهْدِ وَكَهْلاً وَإِذْ عَلَّمْتُكَ الْكِتَابَ

---

103. So when I have proportioned him and breathed into him of My [created] soul, then fall down to him in prostration." [He is] the Exalted above [all] degrees, Owner of the Throne; He places the inspiration of His command upon whom He wills of His servants [He is] the Exalted above [all] degrees, Owner of the Throne; He places the inspiration of His command upon whom He wills of His servants to warn of the Day of Meeting.

104. And she took, in seclusion from them, a screen. Then We sent to her Our Angel, and he represented himself to her as a well-proportioned man. She said, "Indeed, I seek refuge in the Most Merciful from you, [so leave me], if you should be fearing of Allah." He said, "I am only the messenger of your Lord to give you [news of] a pure boy."

105. [The Day] when Allah will say, "O Jesus, Son of Mary, remember My favor upon you and upon your mother when I supported you with the Pure Spirit and you spoke to the people in the cradle and in maturity; and [remember] when I taught you writing and wisdom and the Torah and the Gospel; and when you designed from clay [what was] like the form of a bird with My permission, then you breathed into it, and it became a bird with My permission; and you healed the blind and the leper with My permission; and when you brought forth the dead with My permission; and when I restrained the Children of Israel from [killing] you when you came to them with clear proofs and those who disbelieved among them said, "This is not but obvious magic."

وَالْحِكْمَةَ وَالتَّوْرَاةَ وَالإِنجِيلَ وَإِذْ تَخْلُقُ مِنَ الطِّينِ كَهَيْئَةِ الطَّيْرِ بِإِذْنِي فَتَنفُخُ فِيهَا فَتَكُونُ طَيْرًا بِإِذْنِي وَتُبْرِىءُ الأَكْمَهَ وَالأَبْرَصَ بِإِذْنِي وَإِذْ تُخْرِجُ الْمَوْتَى بِإِذْنِي وَإِذْ كَفَفْتُ بَنِي إِسْرَائِيلَ عَنكَ إِذْ جِئْتَهُمْ بِالْبَيِّنَاتِ فَقَالَ الَّذِينَ كَفَرُواْ مِنْهُمْ إِنْ هَذَا إِلاَّ سِحْرٌ مُّبِينٌ {المائدة/110}

One can realize that in the above ayah the phrase بِإِذْنِي is constantly repeated and emphasized in order to underline this wrong concept of deity given to Isa as that everything is executed with the permission and enablement of Allah ﷻ.

In this regard, one can review this wrong renderings of trinity deviating from pure monotheism, tawhid with the wrong renderings of giving deity to Jibril as the Holy Spirit with his engagements of life, and Isa as due to his performed miracles.

One should remember that everything but everything is with the enablement and permission of Allah ﷻ. Jibril as is the Blessed a'bd of Allah ﷻ and Isa as the Blessed 'abd of Allah ﷻ . Therefore, the Qurān explicitly mentions this mistake of Christians and counsels them as

لَّقَدْ كَفَرَ الَّذِينَ قَالُواْ إِنَّ اللّهَ ثَالِثُ ثَلاَثَةٍ وَمَا مِنْ إِلَهٍ إِلاَّ إِلَهٌ وَاحِدٌ وَإِن لَّمْ يَنتَهُواْ عَمَّا يَقُولُونَ لَيَمَسَّنَّ الَّذِينَ كَفَرُواْ مِنْهُمْ عَذَابٌ أَلِيمٌ [106] {المائدة/73}

يَا أَهْلَ الْكِتَابِ لاَ تَغْلُواْ فِي دِينِكُمْ وَلاَ تَقُولُواْ عَلَى اللّهِ إِلاَّ الْحَقِّ إِنَّمَا الْمَسِيحُ عِيسَى ابْنُ مَرْيَمَ رَسُولُ اللّهِ وَكَلِمَتُهُ أَلْقَاهَا إِلَى مَرْيَمَ وَرُوحٌ مِّنْهُ فَآمِنُواْ بِاللّهِ وَرُسُلِهِ وَلاَ تَقُولُواْ ثَلاَثَةٌ انتَهُواْ خَيْرًا لَّكُمْ إِنَّمَا اللّهُ إِلَهٌ وَاحِدٌ سُبْحَانَهُ أَن يَكُونَ لَهُ وَلَدٌ لَّهُ مَا فِي السَّمَاوَات وَمَا فِي الأَرْضِ وَكَفَى بِاللّهِ وَكِيلاً {النساء/171}

Ismul Azam

The high maqām of Jibril as among other angels refer as the Rûh or Ruhul Qudus is due to their relation with one of Ismul – A'zam of Allah ﷻ as al-Hayy that is the Source of Life and Existence.

In that sense, one can interpret the relation of Isa as and Adam as with Ismul Azam of Allah ﷻ al-Hayy. It can be due to this relation

---

106. They have certainly disbelieved who say, "Allah is the third of three." And there is no god except one God. And if they do not desist from what they are saying, there will surely afflict the disbelievers among them a painful punishment. O People of the Scripture, do not commit excess in your religion or say about Allah except the truth. The Messiah, Jesus, the son of Mary, was but a messenger of Allah and His word which He directed to Mary and a soul [created at a command] from Him. So believe in Allah and His messengers. And do not say, "Three"; desist—it is better for you. Indeed, Allah is but one God. Exalted is He above having a son. To Him belongs whatever is in the heavens and whatever is on the earth. And sufficient is Allah as Dis

of Adam as with this Ismul A'zam that he as is the most inclusive prophets as the father of all humans representing life in population and multiplicity. It can be again to this relation of Isa as with this Ismul Azam that Christians in number today and until the Day of Qiyamah that they would be in multiplicity as mentioned [107] إِذْ قَالَ اللَّهُ يَا عِيسَى إِنِّي مُتَوَفِّيكَ وَرَافِعُكَ إِلَيَّ وَمُطَهِّرُكَ مِنَ الَّذِينَ كَفَرُواْ وَجَاعِلُ الَّذِينَ اتَّبَعُوكَ فَوْقَ الَّذِينَ كَفَرُواْ إِلَى يَوْمِ الْقِيَامَةِ ثُمَّ إِلَيَّ مَرْجِعُكُمْ فَأَحْكُمُ بَيْنَكُمْ فِيمَا كُنتُمْ فِيهِ تَخْتَلِفُونَ {آل عمران/55}

Rasulullah ﷺ is the al-Jami'u as the final and all inclusive prophet of Allah ﷻ. This position is the lead position in front of all the prophets. The risalah of Rasulullah ﷺ is all inlusive of other prophets. the position of Rasulullah ﷺ has the highest before Rabbul Alamin due to his relation ﷺ with all the Names of Allah ﷻ including the all the Ismul Azam.

Rasulullah ﷺ has the relation with the Name of Allah ﷻ as al-Hayy, therefore, this ummah will be in multitudes as mentioned in the hadith of Rasulullah that this ummah would be most in number in the akhirah [4].

Rasulullah ﷺ has the relation with the Name of Allah ﷻ as al-Qayyum, therefore, the position of Rasulullah ﷺ will continue in the afterlife in maqamul mahmud as still saving people from Jahannam as mentioned in the hadith [4].

Rasulullah ﷺ has the relation with Name of Allah ﷻ as al-Wadud, therefore, the title of Rasulullah ﷺ is al-Habib ﷺ, and therefore, Allah ﷻ put the love in creation for this ummah. Therefore, this ummah is best ummah among all as Rasulullah ﷺ has the highest position with Allah ﷻ as al-Habib as mentioned [108] كُنتُمْ خَيْرَ أُمَّةٍ أُخْرِجَتْ لِلنَّاسِ تَأْمُرُونَ بِالْمَعْرُوفِ وَتَنْهَوْنَ عَنِ الْمُنكَرِ وَتُؤْمِنُونَ بِاللَّهِ وَلَوْ آمَنَ أَهْلُ الْكِتَابِ لَكَانَ خَيْرًا لَّهُم مِّنْهُمُ الْمُؤْمِنُونَ وَأَكْثَرُهُمُ الْفَاسِقُونَ {آل عمران/110}

Rasulullah ﷺ has the relation with the Name of Allah ﷻ as and Ar-Rahman, therefore, the Qurān mentions that Rasulullah ﷺ is Rahmatan lil alamin as mentioned [109] {الأنبياء/107} وَمَا أَرْسَلْنَاكَ إِلاَّ رَحْمَةً لِّلْعَالَمِينَ

---

107. [Mention] when Allah said, "O Jesus, indeed I will take you and raise you to Myself and purify you from those who disbelieve and make those who follow you [in submission to Allah alone] superior to those who disbelieve until the Day of Resurrection. Then to Me is your return, and I will judge between you concerning that in which you used to differ.

108. You are the best nation produced [as an example] for mankind. You enjoin what is right and forbid what is wrong and believe in Allah. If only the People of the Scripture had believed, it would have been better for them. Among them are believers, but most of them are defiantly disobedient.

109. And We have not sent you, [O Muhammad], except as a mercy to the worlds.

Rasulullah ﷺ has the relation with the Names of Allah ﷻ as Rauf and ar-Rahim, therefore, the Qurān mentions that Rasulullah is rauf and Rahim for all creation as mentioned [110] لَقَدْ جَاءكُمْ رَسُولٌ مِّنْ أَنفُسِكُمْ عَزِيزٌ عَلَيْهِ مَا عَنِتُّمْ حَرِيصٌ عَلَيْكُم بِالْمُؤْمِنِينَ رَؤُوفٌ رَّحِيمٌ {التوبة/128}

SubhanAllah!

What a High Position and How much we are lucky that we are the uummah of Rasulullah ﷺ!

Alhamdullillahi Allazi Ja'alana min ummati Muhammad al Mustafa, Habib, Rauf, Rahim, and Rahmatan lil Alamin, ﷺ !

Sûrah 18 al-Kahf

[13-10]

Futuwwah

نَحْنُ نَقُصُّ عَلَيْكَ نَبَأَهُم بِالْحَقِّ إِنَّهُمْ فِتْيَةٌ آمَنُوا بِرَبِّهِمْ وَزِدْنَاهُمْ هُدًى [111] {الكهف/13}

قَالُوا سَمِعْنَا فَتًى يَذْكُرُهُمْ يُقَالُ لَهُ إِبْرَاهِيمُ [112] {الأنبياء/60}

When we consider our times and in the past, one can feel the person can be in desperate need of motivation that entails chivalry in the engagements of the deen.

Although there is the prudence of reason, logic and patience, chivalry titled as futuwwah requires always having the active patience of engagements regardless of the people's mockery, discouragement, pessimism, and laziness.

Futuwwah is the disposition of the person even not a second being hopeless from the Fadl, Rahmah and Grace of Allah ﷻ.

In this regard, futuwwah requires sole and unique taslim, tawakkul and taw'fiz to Allah ﷻ.

When people are in their social and world engagements of the norms, futuwwah requires analyzing the reasons, events, and incidents beyond their apparent meanings with their true relation to Rabbul Alamin, al-Basìr, al-Hakìm and as-Samì'.

---

110. There has certainly come to you a Messenger from among yourselves. Grievous to him is what you suffer; [he is] concerned over you and to the believers is kind and merciful.
111. It is We who relate to you, [O Muhammad], their story in truth. Indeed, they were youths who believed in their Lord, and We increased them in guidance.
112. They said, "We heard a young man mention them who is called Abraham."

Futuwwah requires giving constant hope, motivation, encouragement and the soul of revival to the people.

Even if the person of futuwwah can be seen as an outcast with his or
her ideals, the person of futuwwah engages with everything in his or her
primary responsibility to Allah ﷻ.

The person of futuwwah has a special relationship with Allah ﷻ
through I'badah.

Night prayers are the times for the person of futuwwah to discharge
him or herself to Allah ﷻ so that he can be charged and get his energy,
motivation, and hope from al-Baki while dealing with hopeless and
pessimistic people on the earth.

The person of futuwwah has the sweetest time of his or her life when
he or she is in seclusion with Allah ﷻ. In this regard, one can review the
ayahs of the Qurān to realize this private and deep relationship of the
person of futuwwah with Allah ﷻ in the places of seclusions such as in
the prisons as in the case of Yusuf as and his two friends as mentioned [113]

وَدَخَلَ مَعَهُ السِّجْنَ فَتَيَانِ قَالَ أَحَدُهُمَآ إِنِّي أَرَانِي أَعْصِرُ خَمْرًا وَقَالَ الآخَرُ إِنِّي أَرَانِي أَحْمِلُ فَوْقَ رَأْسِي خُبْزًا تَأْكُلُ الطَّيْرُ مِنْهُ نَبِّئْنَا بِتَأْوِيلِهِ إِنَّا نَرَاكَ مِنَ الْمُحْسِنِينَ {يوسف/63}

Or, Ibrahim as turning to Allah ﷻ in different places such as in the
desert or in the fire [114] قَالُوا ابْنُوا لَهُ بُنْيَانًا فَأَلْقُوهُ فِي الْجَحِيمِ {الصافات/97} فَأَرَادُوا بِهِ
كَيْدًا فَجَعَلْنَاهُمُ الْأَسْفَلِينَ {الصافات/98} وَقَالَ إِنِّي ذَاهِبٌ إِلَى رَبِّي سَيَهْدِينِ {الصافات/99}

Or, the futuwwah people of cave-Kahf, having the primary and in
depth relationship with Allah ﷻ in their seclusion as mentioned [115] إِذْ
أَوَى الْفِتْيَةُ إِلَى الْكَهْفِ فَقَالُوا رَبَّنَا آتِنَا مِن لَّدُنكَ رَحْمَةً وَهَيِّئْ لَنَا مِنْ أَمْرِنَا رَشَدًا {الكهف/10}
فَضَرَبْنَا عَلَى آذَانِهِمْ فِي الْكَهْفِ سِنِينَ عَدَدًا {الكهف/11} ثُمَّ بَعَثْنَاهُمْ لِنَعْلَمَ أَيُّ الْحِزْبَيْنِ أَحْصَى
لِمَا لَبِثُوا أَمَدًا {الكهف/12}

Yet, Rasulullah ﷺ was the epitome of all these perfect qualities
as well as being the role model in the field of futuwwah. It was this

---

113. And there entered the prison with him two young men. One of them said, "Indeed, I have
seen myself [in a dream] pressing wine." The other said, "Indeed, I have seen myself carrying
upon my head [some] bread, from which the birds were eating. Inform us of its interpretation;
indeed, we see you to be of those who do good."
114. They said, "Construct for him a furnace and throw him into the burning fire." And they
intended for him a plan, but We made them the most debased. And [then] he said, "Indeed, I
will go to [where I am ordered by] my Lord; He will guide me.
115. [Mention] when the youths retreated to the cave and said, "Our Lord, grant us from
Yourself mercy and prepare for us from our affair right guidance." So We cast [a cover of
sleep] over their ears within the cave for a number of years. Then We awakened them that We
might show which of the two factions was most precise in calculating what [extent] they had
remained in time.

embodiment of futuwwah in Rasulullah 鸞 that made him in seclusive states in the cave or kingdom of Hira.

He 鸞 was contemplated about the problems, injustices, disbelief of his 鸞 people and about all humanity.

The person of futuwwah as realized in the life of Rasulullah 鸞 has this constant worry, concern and care for others beyond limits.

Therefore, Allah 鸞 with the Divine Hikmah as al-Hakìm chooses the people futuwwah with a task and noble responsibility of helping others due to their existent concerns for others.

Rasulullah 鸞 continued and peaked in the maqām of futuwwah during his prophethood.

Although he 鸞 was physically with people but not in seclusion in the cave or kingdom of hira as before, he 鸞 was constantly in the state of futuwwah while among people, in the masjid or at home.

Rasulullah 鸞 was smiling to people. Yet, his maqam with Allah 鸞 in the field of futuwwah compelled him to have the incessant concern of others and yet, he 鸞 was with Allah 鸞 at all times with ihsan.

In one of the occasions to explain this state of his 鸞, he said "If you knew what I knew, you would laugh less and cry a lot. You will leave your businesses, families, children, and run to the mountains," [7] (hadith#:2359). The state of futuwwah was present with Rasulullah 鸞 at all times.

Yet, in this type of futuwwah, Rasulullah 鸞 was teaching the ummah how to ideally implement futuwwah. The implementation of futuwwah for the ummah of Rasulullah 鸞 was being with people at all times with the utmost concern of helping and guiding them to the path of Allah 鸞 with the Divine Fadl and Grace. Yet, at the same being with Allah 鸞 at all times to bear the difficulties of this responsibility of futuwwah giving service to all humans and all creation.

The person of futuwwah does not lose hope.

The person of futuwwah always smiles and gives the people comfort although their internal state can be burning and in fire.

The person of futuwwah engages people, eats and drinks. Yet, he or she has the ultimate concern of accountability of all n'imahs in front of Allah 鸞.

The person of futuwwah does not lose composure, tranquility, and calmness when challenged in a conflict, argument or quarrel. He or she sees everything as a guest on the path of Allah ﷻ and expects all the rewards for these guests from Allah ﷻ.

The person of futuwwah remembers his or her past mistakes or sins constantly. Even, it may be a small mistake that he or she did twenty years ago, he or she still does not forgive himself or herself.

The person of futuwwah does not claim or desire for physical or spiritual privileges. He or she does everything due to the natural state of shukr and hamd to Rabbul Alam'in. He or she sees the service all humanity and creation as part of the expression of shukr and hamd to Allah ﷻ.

If there are times that the person of futuwwah is affected with everyone's overarching pessimistic, lazy and hopeless approaches, he or she tries to immediately collect oneself from people's negative effects. Then, even alone, he or she takes all the challenges even if all the world can be against him or her.

The person of futuwwah follows and applies the teachings of the Qurān and sunnah very carefully and accurately.

May Allah ﷻ make us walk on the path of futuwwah, Amìn!

Sûrah Shua'rah

[77-89]

فَإِنَّهُمْ عَدُوٌّ لِّي إِلَّا رَبَّ الْعَالَمِينَ {الشعراء/77} الَّذِي خَلَقَنِي فَهُوَ يَهْدِينِ {الشعراء/78}
[116] وَالَّذِي هُوَ يُطْعِمُنِي وَيَسْقِينِ {الشعراء/79} وَإِذَا مَرِضْتُ فَهُوَ يَشْفِينِ {الشعراء/80}
وَالَّذِي يُمِيتُنِي ثُمَّ يُحْيِينِ {الشعراء/81} وَالَّذِي أَطْمَعُ أَن يَغْفِرَ لِي خَطِيئَتِي يَوْمَ الدِّينِ
{الشعراء/82} رَبِّ هَبْ لِي حُكْمًا وَأَلْحِقْنِي بِالصَّالِحِينَ {الشعراء/83}

وَاجْعَل لِّي لِسَانَ صِدْقٍ فِي الْآخِرِينَ {الشعراء/84} وَاجْعَلْنِي مِن وَرَثَةِ جَنَّةِ النَّعِيمِ
{الشعراء/85} وَاغْفِرْ لِأَبِي إِنَّهُ كَانَ مِنَ الضَّالِّينَ {الشعراء/86} وَلَا تُخْزِنِي يَوْمَ يُبْعَثُونَ

---

116. Indeed, they are enemies to me, except the Lord of the worlds, Who created me, and He [it is who] guides me. And it is He who feeds me and gives me drink. And when I am ill, it is He who cures me And who will cause me to die and then bring me to life And who I aspire that He will forgive me my sin on the Day of Recompense." [And he said], "My Lord, grant me authority and join me with the righteous.

117. And grant me a reputation of honor among later generations. And place me among the inheritors of the Garden of Pleasure. And forgive my father. Indeed, he has been of those astray. And do not disgrace me on the Day they are [all] resurrected—The Day when there will not benefit [anyone] wealth or children But only one who comes to Allah with a sound heart."

{الشعراء/87} يَوْمَ لَا يَنفَعُ مَالٌ وَلَا بَنُونَ {الشعراء/88} إِلَّا مَنْ أَتَى اللَّهَ بِقَلْبٍ سَلِيمٍ {الشعراء/89}

The Maqam of Khalilullah

One should ask the question how can we achieve the maqam of Khalilullah like Ibrahim as and Rasulullah ﷺ ?

First, it is important to understand the reality of [118] فَإِنَّهُمْ عَدُوٌّ لِّي إِلَّا رَبَّ الْعَالَمِينَ {الشعراء/77}. This is the reality of everything, but everything can be an enemy and opponent and work for the destruction of the person except Allah ﷻ. This is indicated as [119] يَوْمَ يَفِرُّ الْمَرْءُ مِنْ أَخِيهِ {عبس/34} وَأُمِّهِ وَأَبِيهِ {عبس/35} وَصَاحِبَتِهِ وَبَنِيهِ {عبس/36} لِكُلِّ امْرِئٍ مِّنْهُمْ يَوْمَئِذٍ شَأْنٌ يُغْنِيهِ {عبس/37}.

The reality of La ilaha illa Allah indicates this reality.

On a side note, due to the high maqam of Rasulullah ﷺ, La ilaha illa Allah Muhammadan Rasulullah is added as part of one's imān as well. Allah ﷻ has included Rasulullah ﷺ next to this Divine phrase of La ilaha illa Allah.

La ilaha illa Allah and Khaliliyah

How can we embody this reality of La ilaha illa Allah to be a candidate for the maqam of Khalilullah?

In its true and absolute reality, Allah ﷻ has created the person and guided as mentioned [120] الَّذِي خَلَقَنِي فَهُوَ يَهْدِينِ {الشعراء/78}.

In its true and absolute reality, Allah ﷻ gives the sustenance for the physical body and spiritual faculties. Allah ﷻ maintains the stability our body and the environment that needs for this body as mentioned [121] وَالَّذِي هُوَ يُطْعِمُنِي وَيَسْقِينِ {الشعراء/79}.

In its true and absolute reality, Allah ﷻ gives the shifā, recovery and treatment through the means of medicine [122] وَإِذَا مَرِضْتُ فَهُوَ يَشْفِينِ {الشعراء/80}. The case of sickness is specifically mentioned because at the

---

118. Indeed, they are enemies to me, except the Lord of the worlds,
119. On the Day a man will flee from his brother And his mother and his father And his wife and his children, For every man, that Day, will be a matter adequate for him.
120. Who created me, and He [it is who] guides me.
121. And it is He who feeds me and gives me drink.
122. And when I am ill, it is He who cures me

times of sickness, we feel our full weakness and our full dependency on Allah ﷻ. Other times, we can be more in gaflah, heedlessness.

In its true and absolute reality, Allah ﷻ enables the death and resurrection after death as mentioned [123] ﴿الشعراء/18﴾ وَالَّذِي يُمِيتُنِي ثُمَّ يُحْيِينِ.

Then, embodying all takes the person to the maqam and states of Khalilullah at different levels.

After all this how can a person act blind toward All Real Benefactor, the Real Friend, the Real Care Taker, the Real One who the person is constantl dependent on?

Yet, in its true and absolute reality, we as humans cannot appreciate, thank and show gratitude to Allah ﷻ in the reality of in comparison to how much Allah ﷻ does for us. This is mentioned as [124] وَمَا قَدَرُوا اللَّهَ حَقَّ قَدْرِهِ وَالْأَرْضُ جَمِيعًا قَبْضَتُهُ يَوْمَ الْقِيَامَةِ وَالسَّمَاوَاتُ مَطْوِيَّاتٌ بِيَمِينِهِ سُبْحَانَهُ وَتَعَالَى عَمَّا يُشْرِكُونَ ﴿الزمر/76﴾

The real love as popularized in today's language is not in the humanly popular understandings.

The real love for Allah ﷻ entails

due to the One Who did so much for the person and

the person loves the One and

does not displease the One,

Allah ﷻ even a little bit.

Yet, as humans as we can't truly appreciate, thank and show our gratitude to Allah ﷻ, our logical stance requires us constantly showing gratitude and yet at the same time asking forgiveness to Allah ﷻ due to lack and absence of the full and absolute appreciation due to our shortcomings and mistakes as mentioned [125] وَالَّذِي أَطْمَعُ أَن يَغْفِرَ لِي خَطِيئَتِي يَوْمَ الدِّينِ ﴿الشعراء/82﴾.

After this disposition in one's relationship with Allah ﷻ as a potential Khalilullah candidate, one can now ask the means for the help of Allah ﷻ with dua to please Allah ﷻ. This can be such as:

---

123. And who will cause me to die and then bring me to life
124. They have not appraised Allah with true appraisal, while the earth entirely will be [within] His grip on the Day of Resurrection, and the heavens will be folded in His right hand. Exalted is He and high above what they associate with Him.
125. And who I aspire that He will forgive me my sin on the Day of Recompense."

رَبِّ هَبْ لِي حُكْمًا وَأَلْحِقْنِي بِالصَّالِحِينَ [126] {الشعراء/83}

وَاجْعَلْ لِي لِسَانَ صِدْقٍ فِي الْآخِرِينَ {الشعراء/84} وَاجْعَلْنِي مِن وَرَثَةِ جَنَّةِ النَّعِيمِ {الشعراء/85} وَاغْفِرْ لِأَبِي إِنَّهُ كَانَ مِنَ الضَّالِّينَ {الشعراء/86} وَلَا تُخْزِنِي يَوْمَ يُبْعَثُونَ {الشعراء/87} يَوْمَ لَا يَنفَعُ مَالٌ وَلَا بَنُونَ {الشعراء/88} إِلَّا مَنْ أَتَى اللَّهَ بِقَلْبٍ سَلِيمٍ {الشعراء/89}

In this regard, one can and should do good deeds in order to please Allah ﷻ to be the candidate of being Khalilullah.

In that sense, these good deeds can have an outcome of [127] وَاجْعَل لِّي لِسَانَ صِدْقٍ فِي الْآخِرِينَ {الشعراء/84}. Our human nature desires to establish sadaqa-I jariya type remembrance in order to be alive although our physical bodies may be dead. Sadaqa-Jariya establishes this continuous source of good deeds to please Allah ﷻ even though the person may be dead.

Yet, at the same time, it is very easy to be swayed with ostentation and riya of concerns of this world. Therefore, the following part ensures our well ware in the next life but not only this life as [128] وَاجْعَلْنِي مِن وَرَثَةِ جَنَّةِ النَّعِيمِ {الشعراء/85}. Especially, the following ayahs underlines the requirement of ikhlas for all the good actions to be done only to please Allah with a sound heart but not for the temporal beings such as humans as mentioned [129] وَلَا تُخْزِنِي يَوْمَ يُبْعَثُونَ {الشعراء/87} يَوْمَ لَا يَنفَعُ مَالٌ وَلَا بَنُونَ {الشعراء/88} إِلَّا مَنْ أَتَى اللَّهَ بِقَلْبٍ سَلِيمٍ {الشعراء/89}

At the same, one should also ask the well-being of others as part of thanking others they wer the means in one's life. Especially, this is ordered by Allah ﷻ for the ones who did much for the person such as the parents as mentioned [130] وَاغْفِرْ لِأَبِي إِنَّهُ كَانَ مِنَ الضَّالِّينَ {الشعراء/86}.

---

126. [And he said], "My Lord, grant me authority and join me with the righteous. And grant me a reputation of honor among later generations. And place me among the inheritors of the Garden of Pleasure. And forgive my father. Indeed, he has been of those astray. And do not disgrace me on the Day they are [all] resurrected—The Day when there will not benefit [anyone] wealth or children But only one who comes to Allah with a sound heart."

127. And grant me a reputation of honor among later generations.

128. And place me among the inheritors of the Garden of Pleasure.

129. And do not disgrace me on the Day they are [all] resurrected—The Day when there will not benefit [anyone] wealth or children

130. And forgive my father. Indeed, he has been of those astray.

[89]

Qalbun Salīm: Peaceful States of Heart, & Khaliliyah

إِلَّا مَنْ أَتَى اللَّهَ بِقَلْبٍ سَلِيمٍ {الشعراء/89}

When we consider the essence of our pure soul and purpose in life, one should remember that the soul displayed as the spiritual heart or qalb desires the peaceful spiritual states. The words salām, or taslīm, or Islām or Muslim can indicate this reality as derived from the same word.

The peaceful state of the heart is achieved by attaching the heart with only but only Allah ﷻ as mentioned [131] {الشعراء/89} إِلاَّ مَنْ أَتَى اَللَّهَ بِقَلْبٍ سَلِيمٍ.

There are examples among humans who achieved this state of the heart. One of the examples is Ibrahim as as mentioned [132] إِذْ جَاءَ رَبَّهُ بِقَلْبٍ سَلِيمٍ {الصافات/84}.

A person who achieves this level of state of heart can be given a status and title as Khalilullah as mentioned [133] وَمَنْ أَحْسَنُ دِينًا مِّمَّنْ أَسْلَمَ وَجْهَهُ لله وَهُوَ مُحْسِنٌ واتَّبَعَ مِلَّةَ إِبْرَاهِيمَ حَنِيفًا وَاتَّخَذَ اللّهُ إِبْرَاهِيمَ خَلِيلاً {النساء/125}. One can realize that in this ayah to the reach the maqām and level of khaliliyah, the required condition is مِّمَّنْ أَسْلَمَ وَجْهَهُ لله وَهُوَ مُحْسِنٌ. In this regard, the state or maqām of a muhsin or ihsān is complementary with the peaceful state of heart.

In other words, the peaceful state and maqām of the heart is achieved only by attaching the heart but only to Allah ﷻ. This is only accomplished with the state and maqām of ihsān as a muhsin.

One should remember that we get encouraged and proud with our world titles of president, doctor, PhD, MD, chair etc. Yet, these titles are all pseudo and fake and temporary as only valid in the realms of this world as these titles are generated by humans in their value system.

The titles such as khalilullah is given by Allah ﷻ to the person who achieved a lifelong struggle against the internal frictions of nafs and against the external frictions of Shaytān. Moreover, this struggle can be in a society where the person can be alone challenging the norms and values by himself or herself without any humanly recognition or

---

131. But only one who comes to Allah with a sound heart."
132. When he came to his Lord with a sound heart
133. And who is better in religion than one who submits himself to Allah while being a doer of good and follows the religion of Abraham, inclining toward truth? And Allah took Abraham as an intimate friend.

valuation. Oppositely, there can be even the case of humiliation and mockery by others in that society, SubhanAllah!

Therefore, the title of Khalililiyah displays itself after by attaching the heart only but only to Allah ﷻ.

This is a maqām available for ahlullah, for the true and real people of Allah ﷻ. Not all ahlullah can reach to this maqām. Yet, all have the possibility and potential to be the khalilullah at different levels.

When we further analyze the peaceful state of the heart (qalbun salìm) as achieved by attaching the heart to only but only to Allah ﷻ and leading to the maqam of khalilliyah, one can further elaborate on the word Khalil.

Muffassirun [12] elaborated on this word Khalil from the word khullah to indicate a person not asking his or her needs to anyone but except to Allah ﷻ. One can now consider the position of Ibrahim as when he as was challenged as a sole person his society. He as did not ask anyone's help except Allah ﷻ.

A similar case is present with Rasulullah ﷺ that Allah ﷻ mentioned in one of the ayahs of the Qurān as its sabab nuzûl that Allah ﷻ would protect Rasulullah ﷺ that he did not need to have any protection from the sahabas waiting for him outside his house against the possible assassination of the kuffar [1].

In a hadith, Rasulullah ﷺ mentions explicitly that Allah ﷻ took Rasulullah ﷺ as Khalil and Rasulullah ﷺ has the title of Khalilullah as well [4].

As Rasulullah ﷺ has the all-inclusive titles as given by Allah ﷻ compared to other prophets, we are so blessed or lucky as mentioned in the West to be the ummah of Rasulullah ﷺ. We can attain the maqām of khaliliyah through our blessed teacher, Rasulullah ﷺ. This is clearly mentioned in the ayah of the Qurān as [134]

فَلاَ وَرَبِّكَ لاَ يُؤْمِنُونَ حَتَّى يُحَكِّمُوكَ فِيمَا شَجَرَ بَيْنَهُمْ ثُمَّ لاَ يَجِدُواْ فِي أَنفُسِهِمْ حَرَجًا مِّمَّا قَضَيْتَ وَيُسَلِّمُواْ تَسْلِيمًا {النساء/65}

---

134. But no, by your Lord, they will not [truly] believe until they make you, [O Muhammad], judge concerning that over which they dispute among themselves and then find within themselves no discomfort from what you have judged and submit in [full, willing] submission.

إِنَّ اللَّهَ وَمَلَائِكَتَهُ يُصَلُّونَ عَلَى النَّبِيِّ يَا أَيُّهَا الَّذِينَ آمَنُوا صَلُّوا عَلَيْهِ وَسَلِّمُوا تَسْلِيمًا 135 {الأحزاب/56}

وَلَمَّا رَأَى الْمُؤْمِنُونَ الْأَحْزَابَ قَالُوا هَذَا مَا وَعَدَنَا اللَّهُ وَرَسُولُهُ وَصَدَقَ اللَّهُ وَرَسُولُهُ وَمَا زَادَهُمْ إِلَّا إِيمَانًا وَتَسْلِيمًا 136 {الأحزاب/22}

One can again realize the maqām of khaliliyah comes with the peaceful state of the heart (qalbun salim) as achieved by attaching the heart to only but only to Allah ﷻ. Therefore, one should realize the key repeated terms to achieve this maqam as 137 وَيُسَلِّمُواْ تَسْلِيمًا {النساء/56}, وَسَلِّمُوا .وَمَا زَادَهُمْ إِلَّا إِيمَانًا وَتَسْلِيمًا {الأحزاب/22}, and تَسْلِيمًا {الأحزاب/56}.

The above ayahs indicate following the sunnah of Rasulullah ﷺ to achieve and attain the maqam of khaliliyah.

Lut as was on the path of Ibrahim as the Khalil and he was a student of Ibrahim as mentioned as 138 فَآمَنَ لَهُ لُوطٌ وَقَالَ إِنِّي مُهَاجِرٌ إِلَى رَبِّي إِنَّهُ هُوَ الْعَزِيزُ الْحَكِيمُ {العنكبوت/26}.

Yet, as the prophet of Allah ﷻ, Lut as had the maqam of 139 وَإِسْمَاعِيلَ وَلُوطًا آتَيْنَاهُ حُكْمًا وَعِلْمًا and وَالْيَسَعَ وَيُونُسَ وَلُوطًا وَكُلاًّ فَضَّلْنَا عَلَى الْعَالَمِينَ {الأنعام/68} .وَنَجَّيْنَاهُ مِنَ الْقَرْيَةِ الَّتِي كَانَت تَّعْمَلُ الْخَبَائِثَ إِنَّهُمْ كَانُوا قَوْمَ سَوْءٍ فَاسِقِينَ {الأنبياء/47}

---

135. Indeed, Allah confers blessing upon the Prophet, and His angels [ask Him to do so]. O you who have believed, ask [Allah to confer] blessing upon him and ask [Allah to grant him] peace.

136. And when the believers saw the companies, they said, "This is what Allah and His Messenger had promised us, and Allah and His Messenger spoke the truth." And it increased them only in faith and acceptance.

137. But no, by your Lord, they will not [truly] believe until they make you, [O Muhammad], judge concerning that over which they dispute among themselves and then find within themselves no discomfort from what you have judged and submit in [full, willing] submission. But no, by your Lord, they will not [truly] believe until they make you, [O Muhammad], judge concerning that over which they dispute among themselves and then find within themselves no discomfort from what you have judged and submit in [full, willing] submission. And when the believers saw the companies, they said, "This is what Allah and His Messenger had promised us, and Allah and His Messenger spoke the truth." And it increased them only in faith and acceptance.

138. And Lot believed him. [Abraham] said, "Indeed, I will emigrate to [the service of] my Lord. Indeed, He is the Exalted in Might, the Wise

139. ." And Ishmael and Elisha and Jonah and Lot—and all [of them] We preferred over the worlds. And Ishmael and Elisha and Jonah and Lot—and all [of them] We preferred over the worlds.

Juz 20

Sûrah 28 al-Qasas

[4-5]

Following the Clear Guidelines especially at the times of Confusion

إِنَّ فِرْعَوْنَ عَلَا فِي الْأَرْضِ وَجَعَلَ أَهْلَهَا شِيَعًا يَسْتَضْعِفُ طَائِفَةً مِّنْهُمْ يُذَبِّحُ أَبْنَاءهُمْ وَيَسْتَحْيِي نِسَاءهُمْ إِنَّهُ كَانَ مِنَ الْمُفْسِدِينَ {القصص/4} وَنُرِيدُ أَن نَّمُنَّ عَلَى الَّذِينَ اسْتُضْعِفُوا فِي الْأَرْضِ وَنَجْعَلَهُمْ أَئِمَّةً وَنَجْعَلَهُمُ الْوَارِثِينَ ١٤٠ {القصص/5}

It is important to analyze above ayahs with other ayahs of the Qurān al-Karìm such as ¹⁴¹ وَكَانَ فِي الْمَدِينَةِ تِسْعَةُ رَهْطٍ يُفْسِدُونَ فِي الْأَرْضِ وَلاَ يُصْلِحُونَ {النمل/48} قَالُوا تَقَاسَمُوا بِاللَّهِ لَنُبَيِّتَنَّهُ وَأَهْلَهُ ثُمَّ لَنَقُولَنَّ لِوَلِيِّهِ مَا شَهِدْنَا مَهْلِكَ أَهْلِهِ وَإِنَّا لَصَادِقُونَ {النمل/49} وَمَكَرُوا مَكْرًا وَمَكَرْنَا مَكْرًا وَهُم لَا يَشْعُرُونَ {النمل/50}

First, one should understand, there will be always people who would do tyranny, fasad, mischief and chaos on the earth as mentioned with the expressions ¹⁴² وَكَانَ فِي الْمَدِينَةِ تِسْعَةُ رَهْطٍ or إِنَّهُ كَانَ مِنَ الْمُفْسِدِينَ {القصص/4} يُفْسِدُونَ فِي الْأَرْضِ وَلَا يُصْلِحُونَ {النمل/48}.

These tyrannical figures can either be represented as a single embodied figure similar to Firawn as mentioned in the above Sûrah Qasas as إِنَّ فِرْعَوْنَ عَلَا فِي الْأَرْضِ. In this case, this tyranny and oppression can be performed openly and explicitly in the society.

Or, this chaos, fithnah and oppression plans can be executed secretly in their original plan with a group but yet, these planners can claim in public that they are good wishers and they can oath that they are virtuous, moral and ethical. This type of mischief or chaos is mentioned as وَكَانَ فِي الْمَدِينَةِ تِسْعَةُ رَهْطٍ يُفْسِدُونَ فِي الْأَرْضِ.

---

140. Indeed, Pharaoh exalted himself in the land and made its people into factions, oppressing a sector among them, slaughtering their [newborn] sons and keeping their females alive. Indeed, he was of the corrupters. And We wanted to confer favor upon those who were oppressed in the land and make them leaders and make them inheritors

141. And there were in the city nine family heads causing corruption in the land and not amending [its affairs]. They said, "Take a mutual oath by Allah that we will kill him by night, he and his family. Then we will say to his executor, 'We did not witness the destruction of his family, and indeed, we are truthful.'" And they planned a plan, and We planned a plan, while they perceived not.

142. Indeed, Pharaoh exalted himself in the land and made its people into factions, oppressing a sector among them, slaughtering their [newborn] sons and keeping their females alive. Indeed, he was of the corrupters. And there were in the city nine family heads causing corruption in the land and not amending [its affairs].

Yet, in both cases, humans are humans. Creation are all creation whether they are jinn or humans. Even if they help each other in their execution of evil plans, they are still limited, weak and act with the allowance of Allah ﷻ.

Yet, humans are quick to give their judgments as they haste in life as mentioned [143] .خُلِقَ الإِنْسَانُ مِنْ عَجَلٍ سَأُرِيكُمْ آيَاتِي فَلاَ تَسْتَعْجِلُونِ {الأنبياء/37} They really make mistake and lose adab with Allah ﷻ, astagfirullah in evil-seeming incidents, and make blames to qadar, the Divine Decree, astagfirullah.

Yet, Allah ﷻ mentions clearly and explicitly that [144] وَنُرِيدُ أَن نَّمُنَّ عَلَى الَّذِينَ اسْتُضْعِفُوا فِي الْأَرْضِ وَنَجْعَلَهُمْ أَئِمَّةً وَنَجْعَلَهُمُ الْوَارِثِينَ {القصص/5} or وَمَكَرُوا مَكْرًا وَمَكَرْنَا مَكْرًا وَهُمْ لَا يَشْعُرُونَ {النمل/50}. Still, humans hasten, rush and lose adab with Allah ﷻ in their judgment without patience, May Allah ﷻ protect us, Amìn.

One should remember that Allah ﷻ can change anything at any time with the Divine Will as mentioned [145] إِن نَّشَأْ نُنَزِّلْ عَلَيْهِم مِّن السَّمَاء آيَةً فَظَلَّتْ أَعْنَاقُهُمْ لَهَا خَاضِعِينَ {الشعراء/4}

One should also remember that outcome of incidents whether they may look failure, catastrophe, disaster, tragedy, or calamity. Or, if they seem as achievement, triumph, success, victory, or accomplishment are all relative. The true nature of everything is known and controlled by Allah ﷻ Who is al-Alìm, al-Qadìr, al-Jabbar, al-Aliyy and al-Azìm.

This reality is mentioned in the Qurān explicitly as [146] كُتِبَ عَلَيْكُمُ الْقِتَالُ وَهُوَ كُرْهٌ لَّكُمْ وَعَسَى أَن تَكْرَهُواْ شَيْئًا وَهُوَ خَيْرٌ لَّكُمْ وَعَسَى أَن تُحِبُّواْ شَيْئًا وَهُوَ شَرٌّ لَّكُمْ وَاللّهُ يَعْلَمُ وَأَنتُمْ لاَ تَعْلَمُونَ {البقرة/216}

So, what do we do?

It is always important to follow the clear guidelines of the Qurān al-Karìm and the sunnah of Rasulullah ﷺ at all times, especially at the times of chaos, and fithnah where things may be more blurry. It may be difficult to differentiate false from the truth, right from the wrong.

---

143. Man was created of haste. I will show you My signs, so do not impatiently urge Me.
144. And We wanted to confer favor upon those who were oppressed in the land and make them leaders and make them inheritors And they planned a plan, and We planned a plan, while they perceived not.
145. If We willed, We could send down to them from the sky a sign for which their necks would remain humbled.
146. Fighting has been enjoined upon you while it is hateful to you. But perhaps you hate a thing and it is good for you; and perhaps you love a thing and it is bad for you. And Allah Knows, while you know not.

We cannot act as if we know the inner real meanings of things and accordingly make our judgments. No, that is a huge fallacy! Allah ﷻ expects us to act with the clear guidelines of the Qurān and sunnah. Due to our sincere disposition, Allah ﷻ can change anything at any time.

At the times of fithnah or chaos, it is more important to use logic, mind and reason of clear guidelines compared to unclear guidelines of emotions. Yet, making dua to Allah ﷻ while acting with these clear guidelines and expecting results is always the case.

There are many examples of this. For example, Allah ﷻ ordered Rasulullah ﷺ and sahabah at the gazwah of Hudaybiyah to postpone their pilgrimage. Although this was very difficult for the sahabah, Rasulullah ﷺ lead following the order of Allah ﷻ as usual. Then, due to the adab of following the clear guidelines of order from Allah ﷻ, Allah ﷻ turned this incident to one of the highest achievements and triumphs in Islamic history, SubhanAllah!

Today, we don't have Rasulullah ﷺ, al-Hadi ﷺ, with us. Yet, we have the Qurān and sunnah of Rasulullah ﷺ to follow.

Our basic minimum and fundamental teachings are based on the Qurān and sunnah of Rasulullah ﷺ. There is no minimum beyond this point. The Qurān and sunnah of Rasulullah ﷺ are pillars of our creed, aqidah, practice and our religion of Islām.

When we start playing implicitly and explicitly with these basic fundamentals, then the religion is lost. Then, we won't have much difference from ahlu-kitab who did not have any limits of adab with their original sources from Allah ﷻ as they were altering them, hiding them, or making fun of them, Astagfirullah!, May Allah ﷻ protect us and guide us, Amìn!

Sûrah 29 al-ankabût

[45]

الصَّلَاةَ إِنَّ الصَّلَاةَ تَنْهَى عَنِ الْفَحْشَاءِ وَالْمُنكَرِ وَلَذِكْرُ اللَّهِ أَكْبَرُ وَاللَّهُ يَعْلَمُ مَا تَصْنَعُونَ
{العنكبوت/45} [147]

---

147. ecite, [O Muhammad], what has been revealed to you of the Book and establish prayer. Indeed, prayer prohibits immorality and wrongdoing, and the remembrance of Allah is greater. And Allah knows that which you do.

When we analyze the above ayah one can realize that there are different categorizations among the level of believers as mentioned وَلَذِكْرُ اللَّهِ أَكْبَرُ. The comparative form of أَكْبَرُ can indicate this leveling among different Muslims.

One can realize this categorization as mentioned more explicitly in other parts of the Qurān as [148] إِنَّ الْمُسْلِمِينَ وَالْمُسْلِمَاتِ وَالْمُؤْمِنِينَ وَالْمُؤْمِنَاتِ وَالْقَانِتِينَ وَالْقَانِتَاتِ وَالصَّادِقِينَ وَالصَّادِقَاتِ وَالصَّابِرِينَ وَالصَّابِرَاتِ وَالْخَاشِعِينَ وَالْخَاشِعَاتِ وَالْمُتَصَدِّقِينَ وَالْمُتَصَدِّقَاتِ وَالصَّائِمِينَ وَالصَّائِمَاتِ وَالْحَافِظِينَ فُرُوجَهُمْ وَالْحَافِظَاتِ وَالذَّاكِرِينَ اللَّهَ كَثِيرًا وَالذَّاكِرَاتِ أَعَدَّ اللَّهُ لَهُم مَّغْفِرَةً وَأَجْرًا عَظِيمًا {الأحزاب/35}

الَّذِينَ يَقُولُونَ رَبَّنَا إِنَّنَا آمَنَّا فَاغْفِرْ لَنَا ذُنُوبَنَا وَقِنَا عَذَابَ النَّارِ {آل عمران/16} [149] الصَّابِرِينَ وَالصَّادِقِينَ وَالْقَانِتِينَ وَالْمُنفِقِينَ وَالْمُسْتَغْفِرِينَ بِالأَسْحَارِ {آل عمران/17}

One can review above categorizations with the different parts of tazkiya with different means or processes.

True Tazkiya with Rasulullah ﷺ

رَبَّنَا وَابْعَثْ فِيهِمْ رَسُولاً مِّنْهُمْ يَتْلُو عَلَيْهِمْ آيَاتِكَ وَيُعَلِّمُهُمُ الْكِتَابَ وَالْحِكْمَةَ وَيُزَكِّيهِمْ إِنَّكَ أَنتَ الْعَزِيزُ الْحَكِيمُ [150] {البقرة/129}

كَمَا أَرْسَلْنَا فِيكُمْ رَسُولاً مِّنكُمْ يَتْلُو عَلَيْكُمْ آيَاتِنَا وَيُزَكِّيكُمْ وَيُعَلِّمُكُمُ الْكِتَابَ وَالْحِكْمَةَ وَيُعَلِّمُكُم مَّا لَمْ تَكُونُواْ تَعْلَمُونَ [151] {البقرة/151}

---

148. Indeed, the Muslim men and Muslim women, the believing men and believing women, the obedient men and obedient women, the truthful men and truthful women, the patient men and patient women, the humble men and humble women, the charitable men and charitable women, the fasting men and fasting women, the men who guard their private parts and the women who do so, and the men who remember Allah often and the women who do so—for them Allah has prepared forgiveness and a great reward.

149. Those who say, "Our Lord, indeed we have believed, so forgive us our sins and protect Allah witnesses that there is no deity except Him, and [so do] the angels and those of knowledge—[that He is] maintaining [creation] in justice. There is no deity except Him, the Exalted in Might, the Wise.

150. Our Lord, and send among them a messenger from themselves who will recite to them Your verses and teach them the Book and wisdom and purify them. Indeed, You are the Exalted in Might, the Wise."

151. Just as We have sent among you a messenger from yourselves reciting to you Our verses and purifying you and teaching you the Book and wisdom and teaching you that which you did not know.

لَقَدْ مَنَّ اللهُ عَلَى الْمُؤْمِنِينَ إِذْ بَعَثَ فِيهِمْ رَسُولاً مِّنْ أَنفُسِهِمْ يَتْلُو عَلَيْهِمْ آيَاتِهِ وَيُزَكِّيهِمْ
وَيُعَلِّمُهُمُ الْكِتَابَ وَالْحِكْمَةَ وَإِن 152 كَانُواْ مِن قَبْلُ لَفِي ضَلَالٍ مُّبِينٍ {آل عمران/164}

هُوَ الَّذِي بَعَثَ فِي الْأُمِّيِّينَ رَسُولًا مِّنْهُمْ يَتْلُو عَلَيْهِمْ آيَاتِهِ وَيُزَكِّيهِمْ وَيُعَلِّمُهُمُ الْكِتَابَ
وَالْحِكْمَةَ وَإِن كَانُوا مِن قَبْلُ لَفِي ضَلَالٍ مُّبِينٍ {الجمعة/2}

One should remember that we cannot do and understand how to make tazkiya if don't have tazkiya through Rasulullah ﷺ. As humans, we need practical examples in the changing conditions of life. As humans, we are not stable. Everyday, at every hour, at every minute and at every seconds our emotions, engagements and ups & downs change, fluctuate and oscillate. If we don't have a guidance around us from other humans, then it is very difficult to be stable and maintain composure and presence, ihsān in front of Rabbul Alamin.

In today's time, some of the people forget themselves by indulging either in excessive professional work referred as workalcholic. Some indulge in social life or activism. Some indulge in constant talking or lecturing. Yet, it comes become fearful to engage with oneself alone in order to realize this problem of instability. Some people can see others as instable but they may not look at themselves.

Some indulge with self reflection, silence and nature. Yet, since they don't have the true guidance of openings from the Qurān, Rasulullah ﷺ, and required constant ibadah of dhikr of Allah ﷻ through salah and recitation of the Qurān, their self enagements in solitutude can become delusional illusion.

Some indulge themselves with ibadah much without much realizing the need of the purpose of the ibadah leading to tazkiya. Tazkiya without ibadah may not have a value. Ibadah without tazkiya is nothing but a balloon filled with air.

With all these points, if one really reviews the life of Rasulullah ﷺ, one can clearly and explicitly see the inseparable perspectives of I'badah, ilm, and character all with the full embodiment of tazkiya.

---

152. Certainly did Allah confer [great] favor upon the believers when He sent among them a Messenger from themselves, reciting to them His verses and purifying them and teaching them the Book and wisdom, although they had been before in manifest error. It is He who has sent among the unlettered a Messenger from themselves reciting to them His verses and purifying them and teaching them the Book and wisdom—although they were before in clear error—

Therefore, an example like Rasulllah ﷺ is a need for all of us to give practical solutions in our problems related with tazkiya.

Allahumma Ja'alna Min Allazi Tazakka ala sabilika bi Habibika al-Mustafa ﷺ

Falsehood in Self Tazkiya & Following Shaytān

أَلَمْ تَرَ إِلَى الَّذِينَ يُزَكُّونَ أَنفُسَهُمْ بَلِ اللّهُ يُزَكِّي مَن يَشَاء وَلاَ يُظْلَمُونَ فَتِيلاً [153] {النساء/49}

الَّذِينَ يَجْتَنِبُونَ كَبَائِرَ الْإِثْمِ وَالْفَوَاحِشَ إِلَّا اللَّمَمَ إِنَّ رَبَّكَ وَاسِعُ الْمَغْفِرَةِ هُوَ أَعْلَمُ بِكُمْ إِذْ أَنشَأَكُم مِّنَ الْأَرْضِ وَإِذْ أَنتُمْ أَجِنَّةٌ فِي بُطُونِ أُمَّهَاتِكُمْ فَلَا تُزَكُّوا أَنفُسَكُمْ هُوَ أَعْلَمُ بِمَنِ اتَّقَى {النجم/32}

يَا أَيُّهَا الَّذِينَ آمَنُوا لَا تَتَّبِعُوا خُطُوَاتِ الشَّيْطَانِ وَمَن يَتَّبِعْ خُطُوَاتِ الشَّيْطَانِ فَإِنَّهُ يَأْمُرُ بِالْفَحْشَاء وَالْمُنكَرِ وَلَوْلَا فَضْلُ اللَّهِ عَلَيْكُمْ وَرَحْمَتُهُ مَا زَكَا مِنكُم مِّنْ أَحَدٍ أَبَدًا وَلَكِنَّ اللَّهَ يُزَكِّي مَن يَشَاء وَاللَّهُ سَمِيعٌ عَلِيمٌ {النور/21}

One should clearly realize the people who do self-tazkiya are so disgusting. In other words, the people wh constantly engage themselves with their clear false faultlessness but not even consider a possibility a minor fault in themselves but they see others always faulty and wrong are the ones who are disguisting, repulsive and a simple of Shaytān.

These people can call themselves Muslims. Yet, when they always see themselves as flawless, they are not in the required process of tazkiya. A Muslim is a humble and have humility. Humbleness and humility leads the person to realize and see their own faults. This self realization of faults can make the person initiate the process of tazkiya.

---

153. Have you not seen those who claim themselves to be pure? Rather, Allah purifies whom He wills, and injustice is not done to them, [even] as much as a thread [inside a date seed]. Those who avoid the major sins and immoralities, only [committing] slight ones. Indeed, your Lord is vast in forgiveness. He was most knowing of you when He produced you from the earth and when you were fetuses in the wombs of your mothers. So do not claim yourselves to be pure; He is most knowing of who fears Him. O you who have believed, do not follow the footsteps of Satan. And whoever follows the footsteps of Satan—indeed, he enjoins immorality and wrongdoing. And if not for the favor of Allah upon you and His mercy, not one of you would have been pure, ever, but Allah purifies whom He wills, and Allah is Hearing and Knowing.

Source of Kufr and All the Spiritual Diseases Due to Lack of Tazkiya

اذْهَبْ إِلَى فِرْعَوْنَ إِنَّهُ طَغَى {النازعات/17} فَقُلْ هَل لَّكَ إِلَى أَن تَزَكَّى {النازعات/18} وَأَهْدِيَكَ إِلَى رَبِّكَ فَتَخْشَى {النازعات/19} 154 فَأَرَاهُ الْآيَةَ الْكُبْرَى {النازعات/20}

The above ayah is very interesting to ponder. The ayah does not say as "go to Firawn and tell about Allah ﷻ" It mentions before "do you want to do tazkiya?" Why? Because an arrogant person has a problem with tazkiya. Tazkiya requires the realization of this disease of arrogance. Then, accordingly the person can make imān and Islām.

A person who sees him or herself faultless will not be open to listen anything. In this regard, the above initial call to Firawn can indicate the effort of this realization in oneself about the need for tazkiya.

One should remember that Shaytān still did not still realize this root problem of absence of tazkiya. Presence of tazkiya indicate humility and humbleness of realization of one's mistakes. Shaytān still thinks he is right. On the other hand, Adam as did immediately engage in tazkiya by realizing the mistake and made tawbah to Allah ﷻ. This is the main difference. Presence of tazkiya or not.

Tabligh, Dawah & Tazkiya

عَبَسَ وَتَوَلَّى {عبس/1} 155 أَن جَاءهُ الْأَعْمَى {عبس/2} وَمَا يُدْرِيكَ لَعَلَّهُ يَزَّكَّى {عبس/3} أَوْ يَذَّكَّرُ فَتَنفَعَهُ الذِّكْرَى {عبس/4} أَمَّا مَنِ اسْتَغْنَى {عبس/5} فَأَنتَ لَهُ تَصَدَّى {عبس/6} وَمَا عَلَيْكَ أَلَّا يَزَّكَّى {عبس/7} وَأَمَّا مَن جَاءكَ يَسْعَى {عبس/8} وَهُوَ يَخْشَى {عبس/9} فَأَنتَ عَنْهُ تَلَهَّى {عبس/10}

One should remember the initial requirement of tazkiya is the self realization for this need. If someone realizes this need as mentioned وَأَمَّا مَن جَاءكَ يَسْعَى {عبس/8}, then these are the people one can help them to carry them to the next step of Islām, Imān, and Ihsan.

---

154. "Go to Pharaoh. Indeed, he has transgressed. And say to him, 'Would you [be willing to] purify yourself And let me guide you to your Lord so you would fear [Him]?' And he showed him the greatest sign,

155. The Prophet frowned and turned away Because there came to him the blind man, [interrupting]. But what would make you perceive, [O Muhammad], that perhaps he might be purified Or be reminded and the remembrance would benefit him? A s for he who thinks himself without need, To him you give attention. And not upon you [is any blame] if he will not be purified. But as for he who came to you striving [for knowledge] While he fears [Allah], From him you are distracted.

Yet, the ones who are not at this realization such as the Shaytān, Firawn, or the ones like [156] {عبس/5} أَمَّا مَنِ اسْتَغْنَى, there is no purpose of engaging with this people. They need first realization of this need then they can be helped with the Fadl and Grace of Allah ﷻ to the steps of Islām, Imān and Ihsan.

One should observe that one of the benefits of individualistic societies such as the ones in the West, it has many problems. Yet, these people are very close in realization of this problem due to the lifestyles dictating modern seclusion as an outcome of an individualistic society.

Especially, the popular trends of spirituality, meditation, parts of liberalism dictating humbleness and humility are all sources of preparing the minds and hearts of the individuals in the West for the next steps of Islām, Imān, and Ihsan. As one of the new Muslims stated that "tasawwuf or Sufism was the backdoor for me to enter Islām" [5]. This can show that in today's societies one can start with the teachings of ihsan in the beginning for these hearts and minds and go to the teachings of imān and Islām. Especially, when secular minds constantly dictate the need for deductive learning of bottom of approach, the teachings related with ihsan as embodied by the mutassiwin can be the way to go before imān and Islām, Allahu A'lam.

Tazkiya and its Embodiment with Dhikr, Salah

قَدْ أَفْلَحَ مَن تَزَكَّى {الأعلى/14} وَذَكَرَ اسْمَ رَبِّهِ فَصَلَّى [157] {الأعلى/15}

وَلَا تَزِرُ وَازِرَةٌ وِزْرَ أُخْرَى وَإِن تَدْعُ مُثْقَلَةٌ إِلَى حِمْلِهَا لَا يُحْمَلْ مِنْهُ شَيْءٌ وَلَوْ كَانَ ذَا قُرْبَى إِنَّمَا تُنذِرُ الَّذِينَ يَخْشَوْنَ رَبَّهُم بِالْغَيْبِ وَأَقَامُوا الصَّلَاةَ وَمَن تَزَكَّى فَإِنَّمَا يَتَزَكَّى لِنَفْسِهِ وَإِلَى اللَّهِ الْمَصِيرُ {فاطر/18}

One should realize that tazkiya without Dhikr, ibadah and especially without salah is void, empty and will not be embodied by the person. Tazkiya without 'ibadah is not mere than the lofty ideas similar to philosophers' utopia renderings.

---

156. As for he who thinks himself without need,
157. He has certainly succeeded who purifies himself And mentions the name of his Lord and prays. And no bearer of burdens will bear the burden of another. And if a heavily laden soul calls [another] to [carry some of] its load, nothing of it will be carried, even if he should be a close relative. You can only warn those who fear their Lord unseen and have established prayer. And whoever purifies himself only purifies himself for [the benefit of] his soul. And to Allah is the [final] destination.

Tazkiya is the process of both knowledge and practice of the I'badah. Salah opens the door to understand and embody all the teachings of tazkiya such as patience, discipline, sakina, faqr, ajz, and all others. Similarly other 'ibadah have their own critical role to implement the teachings of tazkiya.

Tazkiya and its Embodiment with Halāl and Avodience of Haram ---Fiqh

Practical Examples of Tazkiya with Fiqh

فَإِن لَّمْ تَجِدُوا فِيهَا أَحَدًا فَلَا تَدْخُلُوهَا حَتَّى يُؤْذَنَ لَكُمْ وَإِن قِيلَ لَكُمُ ارْجِعُوا فَارْجِعُوا هُوَ أَزْكَى لَكُمْ وَاللَّهُ بِمَا تَعْمَلُونَ عَلِيمٌ 158 {النور/28} لَيْسَ عَلَيْكُمْ جُنَاحٌ أَن تَدْخُلُوا بُيُوتًا غَيْرَ مَسْكُونَةٍ فِيهَا مَتَاعٌ لَّكُمْ وَاللَّهُ يَعْلَمُ مَا تُبْدُونَ وَمَا تَكْتُمُونَ {النور/29} قُل لِّلْمُؤْمِنِينَ يَغُضُّوا مِنْ أَبْصَارِهِمْ وَيَحْفَظُوا فُرُوجَهُمْ ذَلِكَ أَزْكَى لَهُمْ إِنَّ اللَّهَ خَبِيرٌ بِمَا يَصْنَعُونَ {النور/30}

وَإِذَا طَلَّقْتُمُ النِّسَاء فَبَلَغْنَ أَجَلَهُنَّ فَلاَ تَعْضُلُوهُنَّ أَن يَنكِحْنَ أَزْوَاجَهُنَّ إِذَا تَرَاضَوْاْ بَيْنَهُم بِالْمَعْرُوفِ ذَلِكَ يُوعَظُ بِهِ مَن كَانَ مِنكُمْ يُؤْمِنُ بِاللّهِ وَالْيَوْمِ الآخِرِ ذَلِكُمْ أَزْكَى لَكُمْ وَأَطْهَرُ وَاللّهُ يَعْلَمُ وَأَنتُمْ لاَ تَعْلَمُونَ {البقرة/232}

One should remember that having adab and respect with the rulings of fiqh as the guidelines of halal and haram can take the person another level of tazkiya. A person who is not careful with these guidelenes as primarily outlined by the Qurān and sunnah Rasulullah ﷺ cannot truly be on the guidance with tazkiya.

Above ayahs are some example from the life instances as avoidance from looking into haram, asking permission to enter to a house or following certain non-oppressive etiquettes in the difficult and disturbing cases of divorce are all required parts of the tazkiya when one should abide fiqh rulings on the path of the tazkiyatul nafs.

---

158. And if you do not find anyone therein, do not enter them until permission has been given you. And if it is said to you, "Go back," then go back; it is purer for you. And Allah is Knowing of what you do. There is no blame upon you for entering houses not inhabited in which there is convenience for you. And Allah knows what you reveal and what you conceal. Tell the believing men to reduce [some] of their vision and guard their private parts. That is purer for them. Indeed, Allah is Acquainted with what they do. And when you divorce women and they have fulfilled their term, do not prevent them from remarrying their [former] husbands if they agree among themselves on an acceptable basis. That is instructed to whoever of you believes in Allah and the Last Day. That is better for you and purer, and Allah knows and you know not.

Tazkiya leading to reward

جَنَّاتُ عَدْنٍ تَجْرِي مِن تَحْتِهَا الأَنْهَارُ خَالِدِينَ فِيهَا وَذَلِكَ جَزَاء مَن تَزَكَّى 159 {طه/76}

One should realize that the reward of engagement with oneself with the above processes of tazkiya can make the person enter Jannah with the Fadl and Rahmah of Allah ﷻ as mentioned وَذَلِكَ جَزَاء مَن تَزَكَّى.

In other words, one can say that the purpose of this life is tazkiyatul nafs. One call this as the real purpose. Or, it is the real struggle, jihad of the nafs.

On the opposite, if one does not engage oneself with this real purpose with a true process, then all the efforts can be nullified.

A person who can externality dedicate oneself to I'badah but yet absence of tazkiyatul nafs with these spiritual diseases as expected as the outcome of this I'badah can still go to Jahannam, May Allah ﷻ protect us. One can remember the hadith of the Rasulullah ﷺ about a woman who is the worshipper of God going to hellfire due to not feeding the cat [4]. A person with the atom size of an kibir, arrogance in their heart going to Jahannam [7] (hadith #91). These two cases can indicate the gadab of Allah ﷻ. May Allah ﷻ protect us, Amìn!

One can also think the opposite of a person who is considered as in dalalah, not knowing Allah ﷻ truly but going behind their whimsical delusional thoughts and ideas about Allah ﷻ as their religion. This can indicate the dalalah. May Allah ﷻ protect us, Amìn!

These two categories of magdubi and dalalah are mentioned as 160 اهدِنَا الصِّرَاطَ المُسْتَقِيمَ {الفاتحة/6} صِرَاطَ الَّذِينَ أَنعَمتَ عَلَيهِمْ غَيرِ المَغضُوبِ عَلَيهِمْ وَلاَ الضَّالِّينَ {الفاتحة/7}

One should know that the people who did tazkiyatul nafs will not be in Jahannam with the Fadl and Rahmah of Allah ﷻ.

Yet, the ones who are in Jahannam will enter punishment in that state of absence of tazkiyatul nafs as mentioned وَلاَ يُزَكِّيهِمْ as mentioned in 161

---

159. Gardens of perpetual residence beneath which rivers flow, wherein they abide eternally. And that is the reward of one who purifies himself.

160. Indeed, those who disbelieve—it is all the same for them whether you warn them or do not warn them—they will not believe.

161. Indeed, those who exchange the covenant of Allah and their [own] oaths for a small price will have no share in the Hereafter, and Allah will not speak to them or look at them on the Day of Resurrection, nor will He purify them; and they will have a painful punishment.

إِنَّ الَّذِينَ يَشْتَرُونَ بِعَهْدِ اللّهِ وَأَيْمَانِهِمْ ثَمَنًا قَلِيلاً لاَ خَلاَقَ لَهُمْ فِي الآخِرَةِ وَلاَ يُكَلِّمُهُمُ اللّهُ وَلاَ يَنظُرُ إِلَيْهِمْ يَوْمَ الْقِيَامَةِ وَلاَ يُزَكِّيهِمْ وَلَهُمْ عَذَابٌ أَلِيمٌ {آل عمران/77}

May Allah ﷻ protect us, Amin!

Tazkiya for Children

فَانطَلَقَا حَتَّى إِذَا لَقِيَا غُلاَمًا فَقَتَلَهُ قَالَ أَقَتَلْتَ نَفْسًا زَكِيَّةً بِغَيْرِ نَفْسٍ لَّقَدْ جِئْتَ شَيْئًا نُّكْرًا 162 {الكهف/74}

فَأَرَدْنَا أَن يُبْدِلَهُمَا رَبُّهُمَا خَيْرًا مِّنْهُ زَكَاةً وَأَقْرَبَ رُحْمًا 163 {الكهف/81}

One should remember that the children are in the pure, natural and innate state of tazkiya as mentioned نَفْسًا زَكِيَّة.

Yet, when they become adults they have their own preferences going into either to the path of tazkiya or gadab or dalalah.

At another perspective, even children can have tazkiya before puberty as mentioned نَفْسًا زَكِيَّة. Yet, there can be also the better ones among children as mentioned خَيْرًا مِّنْهُ زَكَاةً.

In this regard, if our purpose of existence is due to our tazkiyatul nafs, then a child void of tazkiyatul nafs can be a source of grief and sorrow in this life and afterlife.

Therefore, as a Mercy, Fadl, and Grace from Rabbul Alamin, death of a this type of child can be mercy both for the parents and the child him or herself. It is a mercy for the parents that they see the sorrow of the absence of tazkiyatul nafs in their children with implicit and explicit kufr to Allah ﷻ and to the parents in the form of gratitude. It is a mercy for the children that if he or she dies before puberty, then he or she can be with their parents in the afterlife in Jannah, InshAllah.

Yet, Allah ﷻ is so merciful that Allah ﷻ gives another child to the parents after the loss of their child.

Yet, in all above renderings of theodicy, when the person does not know these hikmahs, they start blaming God, without adab with Allah

---

162. So they set out, until when they met a boy, al-Khidr killed him. [Moses] said, "Have you killed a pure soul for other than [having killed] a soul? You have certainly done a deplorable thing."

163. So we intended that their Lord should substitute for them one better than him in purity and nearer to mercy.

🌸. When adab is gone, tazkiya is gone. When tazkiya is gone, the real purpose of existence is misplaced and terminated.

May Allah 🕮 protect us, Amìn!

Tazkiya of Food

وَكَذَلِكَ بَعَثْنَاهُمْ لِيَتَسَاءلُوا بَيْنَهُمْ قَالَ قَائِلٌ مِّنْهُمْ كَمْ لَبِثْتُمْ قَالُوا لَبِثْنَا يَوْمًا أَوْ بَعْضَ يَوْمٍ قَالُوا رَبُّكُمْ أَعْلَمُ بِمَا لَبِثْتُمْ فَابْعَثُوا أَحَدَكُم بِوَرِقِكُمْ هَذِهِ إِلَى الْمَدِينَةِ فَلْيَنظُرْ أَيُّهَا أَزْكَى طَعَامًا فَلْيَأْتِكُم بِرِزْقٍ مِّنْهُ وَلْيَتَلَطَّفْ وَلَا يُشْعِرَنَّ بِكُمْ أَحَدًا 164 {الكهف/19}

One should remember that the type of food that we eat has an effect on us in implementing the process of tazkiyatul nafs. The phrase فَلْيَنظُرْ أَيُّهَا أَزْكَى طَعَامًا فَلْيَأْتِكُم بِرِزْقٍ مِّنْهُ can indicate this constant effort of finding and searching for the food that would be clean, organic, pure, and halal that would support the establishment of tazkiya in oneself.

Here in the ayahs, it is interesting to note that when these youth wake up from a long sleep, they don't gabble or find food immediately. They have a lot of concerns of hiding, fear, having no money etc. Yet, among all these concerns, one can think why they care about a clean food. SubhanAllah, yet, they still put an effort for finding the food that would be helpful for their tazkiya as mentioned فَلْيَنظُرْ أَيُّهَا أَزْكَى طَعَامًا فَلْيَأْتِكُم بِرِزْقٍ مِّنْهُ.

Zakah as the Tazkiya

خُذْ مِنْ أَمْوَالِهِمْ صَدَقَةً تُطَهِّرُهُمْ وَتُزَكِّيهِم بِهَا وَصَلِّ عَلَيْهِمْ إِنَّ صَلَاتَكَ سَكَنٌ لَّهُمْ وَاللَّهُ سَمِيعٌ عَلِيمٌ 165 {التوبة/103}

One should remember that zakah is a word derived from the tazkiya. A lot of times our own attachements to the wealth prevents us to implement the teachings of tazkiya against the spiritual diseases such as attachment to the worldly life as opposite to zuhd.

---

164. And similarly, We awakened them that they might question one another. Said a speaker from among them, "How long have you remained [here]?" They said, "We have remained a day or part of a day." They said, "Your Lord is most knowing of how long you remained. So send one of you with this silver coin of yours to the city and let him look to which is the best of food and bring you provision from it and let him be cautious. And let no one be aware of you.

165. Take, [O, Muhammad], from their wealth a charity by which you purify them and cause them increase, and invoke [Allah's blessings] upon them. Indeed, your invocations are reassurance for them. And Allah is Hearing and Knowing.

Yet, zakah is the form 'ibadah that builds in the person the notion and character of detachment from everything especially from the wealth of a person that gives the person the feelings of safety, security, power and authority towards others. SubhanAllah, if one think the life of Rasulullah ﷺ, he ﷺ was always in the practice of emptying everything minutely or hourly at most. He ﷺ did not leave in his overnight as the embodiment of this detachment.

He ﷺ did immediately rush to his home after salah to disritbute a wealth that came in the day time so that it did not stay in his house. SubhanAllah, this is Rasulullah ﷺ as our model and this is us!

Allahumma Ja'alna attabiu sunnatu Habibika Rasulullah ﷺ fi kulli makān, fi kulli ān, acilata wa ajila, Amìn!

Juz 22

Sûrah 33 al-Ahzāb

[53]

يَا أَيُّهَا الَّذِينَ آمَنُوا لَا تَدْخُلُوا بُيُوتَ النَّبِيِّ إِلَّا أَن يُؤْذَنَ لَكُمْ إِلَى طَعَامٍ غَيْرَ نَاظِرِينَ إِنَاهُ وَلَكِنْ إِذَا دُعِيتُمْ فَادْخُلُوا فَإِذَا طَعِمْتُمْ فَانتَشِرُوا وَلَا مُسْتَأْنِسِينَ لِحَدِيثٍ إِنَّ ذَلِكُمْ كَانَ يُؤْذِي النَّبِيَّ فَيَسْتَحْيِي مِنكُمْ وَاللَّهُ لَا يَسْتَحْيِي مِنَ الْحَقِّ وَإِذَا سَأَلْتُمُوهُنَّ مَتَاعًا فَاسْأَلُوهُنَّ مِن وَرَاء حِجَابٍ ذَلِكُمْ أَطْهَرُ لِقُلُوبِكُمْ وَقُلُوبِهِنَّ وَمَا كَانَ لَكُمْ أَن تُؤْذُوا رَسُولَ اللَّهِ وَلَا أَن تَنكِحُوا أَزْوَاجَهُ مِن بَعْدِهِ أَبَدًا إِنَّ ذَلِكُمْ كَانَ عِندَ اللَّهِ عَظِيمًا 166 {الأحزاب/53}

Haya is embodied by Rasulullah ﷺ as mentioned فَيَسْتَحْيِي مِنكُمْ . Haya requires when a person does not like something, he or she still does not openly express his or her dislike.

In this regard, haya has a very strong relationship with patience.

A person of haya talks when it is really necessary. A person of haya is in the state and maqam of the ihsan, in the presence of Allah ﷻ.

---

166. O you who have believed, do not enter the houses of the Prophet except when you are permitted for a meal, without awaiting its readiness. But when you are invited, then enter; and when you have eaten, disperse without seeking to remain for conversation. Indeed, that [behavior] was troubling the Prophet, and he is shy of [dismissing] you. But Allah is not shy of the truth. And when you ask [his wives] for something, ask them from behind a partition. That is purer for your hearts and their hearts. And it is not [conceivable or lawful] for you to harm the Messenger of Allah or to marry his wives after him, ever. Indeed, that would be in the sight of Allah an enormity.

He or she bears and endures people's often belligerent, rude and aggressive behaviors.

He or she does not respond in the coarse manner and treatments like others.

A person of haya maintains silence most of the time. He or she keeps the effect of broken heartedness in themselves instead of lashing out. Even, he or she may not ask justice in the self-related matters. Although the legal-fiqh rulings give the allowance of seeking justice and fairness in self-related engagements, he or she does not take even this permission of the legal rulings.

In all these engagements, when the person upholds this quality, Allah ﷻ defends this person against all injustices, unfairness, rude and belligerent behaviors and attitudes as mentioned وَاللهُ لَا يَسْتَحْيِي مِنَ الْحَقِّ.

Today, the term haya and its applications almost are getting lost. There are very few people who are try to implement this teaching.

In today's society, the notions of fighting for one's rights can make the individuals aggressive, rude, belligerent and make them alienated from the concept of haya.

Haya becomes nowadays a frowned upon quality where the weak or abused can uphold.

Sometimes, the word haya is translated as modesty. Then, people associate this word with the externality, especially how one dresses. Then, this word becomes a tag especially for women among Muslims.

On a negative note, some Westerns who knows some Arabic can argue and translate this word in their framework of introvert, a person who is shy "reserved or having or showing nervousness or timidity in the company of other people," [6].

Yet, this approach is very wrong and reductionist renderings of the notion of haya. Because this notion is not anymore almost not present in our present societies. People do not witness and exemplify of this concept. Especially, in the West, introverts can be tagged some type of medical disorder.

A person of haya expects all the outcomes of his or her renderings from Allah ﷻ. A person of haya does not act like others in the norms of West of one-to-one mind or psychology related expectations. A person of haya has wisdom-hikmah and expects all the outcomes from Allah ﷻ.

A person of haya is hurt, becomes sad and disturbed. Yet, he or she immediately turns to Allah ﷻ in all of his or her internal complaints.

This is mentioned for Yaqub as as one of the embodiment of haya as [167]

قَالَ إِنَّمَا أَشْكُو بَثِّي وَحُزْنِي إِلَى اللّهِ وَأَعْلَمُ مِنَ اللّهِ مَا لاَ تَعْلَمُونَ {يوسف/86}.

A person of haya even does not make rude and belligerent people uncomfortable in their engagements. He or she says and embodies "salam", peace, smiles and maintains the silence.

In this disposition of hikmah, the party of rude and belligerents may have the natural breezes of embarrassment. Although he or she is treating the person of haya in a rude manner, the person of haya still maintains composure, niceness and solemnness.

In this regard, the person of haya has a very transformative effect to the people around him or her. When people spend time with the person of haya, they can feel his or her comforting presence.

May Allah ﷻ make us from the person of haya, Amìn!

Sûrah 36 Yasin

[12]

إِنَّا نَحْنُ نُحْيِي الْمَوْتَى وَنَكْتُبُ مَا قَدَّمُوا وَآثَارَهُمْ وَكُلَّ شَيْءٍ أَحْصَيْنَاهُ فِي إِمَامٍ مُبِينٍ [168]
{يس/12}

The word āthār is a very interesting to analyze. In today's modern times, one of the secular virtuous goals and aims in life is to leave memories, works or actions behind that people can remember the person in a good way. This motivation is increasingly becoming popular especially in the avenues of people separating Allah ﷻ in their lives as this should be the center of aim or goal in one's short life. Yet, this type of motivation excluding Allah ﷻ in goal life in life is oriented towards achieving the results without being much careful about the means. One of the main motivation and expectation of the person can be receiving satisfaction due to recognition and applaud of others.

Yet, for the real purpose of life for a Muslim, the person is encouraged to follow the āthār of Rasulullah ﷺ and all the āthār of other anbiya as instructed in the Qurān and by Rasulullah ﷺ. Then, the person is encouraged to strive and struggle to leave āthār as sadaqa-i

---

167. He said, "I only complain of my suffering and my grief to Allah, and I know from Allah that which you do not know.

168. Indeed, it is We who bring the dead to life and record what they have put forth and what they left behind, and all things We have enumerated in a clear register.

jariya as mentioned by Rasulullah ﷺ [7] (hadith # 1631). Even though the person dies, this āthār in the form of sadaqa-i Jariya can continue on the behalf of the person as amalu salih, good or virtuous actions in order to please Allah ﷻ.

In this perspective of a Muslim as suggested by Rasulullah ﷺ, the recognition by people and even the results are not important. Although the person strives to fulfill all the means and reasons of causality to be successful to achieve the end results with the Fadl and Grace of Allah ﷻ. Yet, if it does not work out, Allah ﷻ still can give the person the reward of their achievement according to their intention primarily and the struggle that they put in this engagement secondarily.

In this regard, recognition or expecting encouragement from people is not important or even it may become dangerous as a possible source of distraction. Yet, the person should struggle as much as possible to leave āthār in order to please Allah ﷻ as encouraged by al-Habìb, Rasulullah [7] (hadith #1631). The hadith mentions three specific categories. One is an 'ilm, knowledge to be benefitted by others. This can be in the form of books that people can read constantly for the consecutive generations. Or, the students who were trained or taught that they continue to teach others for the consecutive generations. The second category is raising children that their offspring continue to do amalu salih for the consecutive generations. The third category is a waqf or a non-for profit entity that humanity continuously benefit for the consecutive generations [7] (hadith #1631).

In all these engagements, the ayah mentions, all these deeds, āthār are being recorded regardless of being virtuous or not that everyone will be accountable in front of Allah ﷻ in all these efforts and engagements.

The Real Āthār and the Real People of Āthār

وَقَفَّيْنَا عَلَى آثَارِهِم بِعَيسَى ابْنِ مَرْيَمَ مُصَدِّقًا لِّمَا بَيْنَ يَدَيْهِ مِنَ التَّوْرَاةِ وَآتَيْنَاهُ الإِنجِيلَ فِيهِ
هُدًى وَنُورٌ وَمُصَدِّقًا لِّمَا بَيْنَ يَدَيْهِ مِنَ التَّوْرَاةِ وَهُدًى وَمَوْعِظَةً لِّلْمُتَّقِينَ 169 {المائدة/46}

---

169. And We sent, following in their footsteps, Jesus, the son of Mary, confirming that which came before him in the Torah; and We gave him the Gospel, in which was guidance and light and confirming that which preceded it of the Torah as guidance and instruction for the righteous Then We sent following their footsteps Our messengers and followed [them] with Jesus, the son of Mary, and gave him the Gospel. And We placed in the hearts of those who followed him compassion and mercy and monasticism, which they innovated; We did not prescribe it for them except [that they did so] seeking the approval of Allah. But they did not observe it with due observance. So We gave the ones who believed among them their reward, but many of them are defiantly disobedient.

ثُمَّ قَفَّيْنَا عَلَى آثَارِهِم بِرُسُلِنَا وَقَفَّيْنَا بِعِيسَى ابْنِ مَرْيَمَ وَآتَيْنَاهُ الْإِنجِيلَ وَجَعَلْنَا فِي قُلُوبِ الَّذِينَ اتَّبَعُوهُ رَأْفَةً وَرَحْمَةً وَرَهْبَانِيَّةً ابْتَدَعُوهَا مَا كَتَبْنَاهَا عَلَيْهِمْ إِلَّا ابْتِغَاءَ رِضْوَانِ اللَّهِ فَمَا رَعَوْهَا حَقَّ رِعَايَتِهَا فَآتَيْنَا الَّذِينَ آمَنُوا مِنْهُمْ أَجْرَهُمْ وَكَثِيرٌ مِّنْهُمْ فَاسِقُونَ {الحديد/27}

When we analyze the ayahs above, Allah ﷻ mentions that there has been always ideal āthār to follow as instructed by Allah ﷻ through teachings of the prophets with the revelations from Allah ﷻ. These prophets can be considered similar to the flagmen showing at each time the true and real āthār that one should understand, follow and accordingly transmit to others for the next generations.

These āthār were not only memories or motivations for personal satisfactions but they have been always the unchanging pillars of guidance and light for the ones who follow them as mentioned هُدًى وَنُورٌ.

Allah ﷻ with the Divine Fadl and Mercy always makes these true and real āthār available and present at all generations at all times as repeatedly mentioned مُصَدِّقًا لِّمَا بَيْنَ يَدَيْهِ.

In other words, when people claim and show off with their identity such as their belongings of a religion such as Christianity, Judaism and even Islām, Allah ﷻ mentions and emphasizes that these true and real pearls and diamonds of āthār have been always present as mentioned [170] آمَنَ or وَقَفَّيْنَا عَلَى آثَارِهِم بِعِيسَى ابْنِ مَرْيَمَ مُصَدِّقًا لِّمَا بَيْنَ يَدَيْهِ مِنَ التَّوْرَاةِ وَآتَيْنَاهُ الْإِنجِيلَ الرَّسُولُ بِمَا أُنزِلَ إِلَيْهِ مِن رَّبِّهِ وَالْمُؤْمِنُونَ كُلٌّ آمَنَ بِاللَّهِ وَمَلَائِكَتِهِ وَكُتُبِهِ وَرُسُلِهِ لَا نُفَرِّقُ بَيْنَ أَحَدٍ مِّن رُّسُلِهِ وَقَالُوا سَمِعْنَا وَأَطَعْنَا غُفْرَانَكَ رَبَّنَا وَإِلَيْكَ الْمَصِيرُ {البقرة/285}

It is interesting to realize that a person of āthār, for example Musa as, follows another person of āthār ,Khidr as mentioned in [171] قَالَ ذَلِكَ مَا كُنَّا نَبْغِ فَارْتَدَّا عَلَى آثَارِهِمَا قَصَصًا {الكهف/64}. This shows that the real people of āthār are always alert and vigilant about any signs to follow. They never claim and assert the dispositions of arrogance as "I am the person of āthār that I needed to be followed." This is another teaching point from the people of āthār for the lowly people like us. When someone follow us, we think ourselves to be at the highest level of guidance with arrogance. When people follow us, we stop following the people of āthār and any teaching that can include genuine teachings from Allah ﷻ and

---

170. The Messenger has believed in what was revealed to him from his Lord, and [so have] the believers. All of them have believed in Allah and His angels and His books and His messengers, [saying], "We make no distinction between any of His messengers." And they say, "We hear and we obey. [We seek] Your forgiveness, our Lord, and to You is the [final] destination."

171. [Moses] said, "That is what we were seeking." So they returned, following their footprints.

Rasulullah ﷺ. Yet, the true and real people of āthār are followed but yet, they themselves follow when they see a sign or another person of āthār, SubhanAllah! Allahumma Ja'alna Minhum!, Amìn!

The Unsound Āthār and the Real People of Āthār

فَلَعَلَّكَ بَاخِعٌ نَّفْسَكَ عَلَى آثَارِهِمْ إِن لَّمْ يُؤْمِنُوا بِهَذَا الْحَدِيثِ أَسَفًا 172 {الكهف/6}

When the people of āthār encounter with the people who are following unsound or unreal āthār, then they engage with them with the concerns of worry and care to explain them about their illusions and lifelong failures if they don't change their dispositions with thinking, reflection and taking advices from the real people of āthār.

The primary example of this Rasulullah ﷺ as the person of the lead of the real people of āthār. He ﷺ had the utmost worry and concern who were wasting their lives for minute and petty goals thinking that they were following a real āthār. Realizing this, Rasulullah ﷺ took this responsibility of care and worry fully on himself ﷺ. His worry before formal prophethood was this ﷺ. His embodiment of this worry continued and peaked after prophethood with the Divine assignment of reminding people about the real āthār in life.

One should know that when a person is worried and concerned about something, Allah ﷻ assigns that person for that duty as one of the principles of sunnatullah. In this regard, Rasulullah ﷺ had the highest concern of worry and care for all humanity before prophethood. With the unchanging conditions of sunnatullah, Allah ﷻ bestowed on Rasulullah ﷺ this Divine yet difficult task of messengership. Rasulullah ﷺ has been given the lead messengership and prophethood due to his highest and utmost concern for all humanity and even for all creation as mentioned as{الأنبياء/107} وَمَا أَرْسَلْنَاكَ 173 إِلاَّ رَحْمَةً لِّلْعَالَمِينَ

---

172. Then perhaps you would kill yourself through grief over them, [O Muhammad], if they do not believe in this message, [and] out of sorrow.

173. And We have not sent you, [O Muhammad], except as a mercy to the worlds. There has certainly come to you a Messenger from among yourselves. Grievous to him is what you suffer; [he is] concerned over you and to the believers is kind and merciful.

لَقَدْ جَاءكُمْ رَسُولٌ مِّنْ أَنفُسِكُمْ عَزِيزٌ عَلَيْهِ مَا عَنِتُّمْ حَرِيصٌ عَلَيْكُم بِالْمُؤْمِنِينَ رَؤُوفٌ رَّحِيمٌ {التوبة/128}

One can always ask to the people who are in the engagements of unsound āthār to show their proof as mentioned [174] قُلْ أَرَأَيْتُم مَّا تَدْعُونَ مِن دُونِ اللَّهِ أَرُونِي مَاذَا خَلَقُوا مِنَ الْأَرْضِ أَمْ لَهُمْ شِرْكٌ فِي السَّمَاوَاتِ اِئْتُونِي بِكِتَابٍ مِّن قَبْلِ هَذَا أَوْ أَثَارَةٍ مِّنْ عِلْمٍ إِن كُنتُمْ صَادِقِينَ {الأحقاف/4}

In this regard, there is a clear real āthar by the prophets sent by Allah ﷻ. On the other hand, there is a very logical question and confrontation mentioned to the people of unsound āthār as اِئْتُونِي بِكِتَابٍ مِّن قَبْلِ هَذَا أَوْ أَثَارَةٍ مِّنْ عِلْمٍ إِن كُنتُمْ صَادِقِينَ.

The Endless and Void Struggle of People Following the Fake Āthār

أَوَلَمْ يَسِيرُوا فِي الْأَرْضِ فَيَنظُرُوا كَيْفَ كَانَ عَاقِبَةُ الَّذِينَ مِن قَبْلِهِمْ كَانُوا أَشَدَّ مِنْهُمْ قُوَّةً وَأَثَارُوا الْأَرْضَ وَعَمَرُوهَا أَكْثَرَ مِمَّا عَمَرُوهَا وَجَاءتْهُمْ رُسُلُهُم بِالْبَيِّنَاتِ فَمَا كَانَ اللَّهُ لِيَظْلِمَهُمْ وَلَكِن كَانُوا أَنفُسَهُمْ يَظْلِمُونَ [175] {الروم/9}

أَفَلَمْ يَسِيرُوا فِي الْأَرْضِ فَيَنظُرُوا كَيْفَ كَانَ عَاقِبَةُ الَّذِينَ مِن قَبْلِهِمْ كَانُوا أَكْثَرَ مِنْهُمْ وَأَشَدَّ قُوَّةً وَآثَارًا فِي الْأَرْضِ فَمَا أَغْنَى عَنْهُم مَّا كَانُوا يَكْسِبُونَ {غافر/82}

When we analyze the above ayahs, one can really realize the endless and much struggle of people who spent all their life thinking that they are on the genuine path of āthār but yet, they have been all nullified, terminated and useless, unfortunately. One can realize the expression that it strongly emphasizes their worldly achievements with building, bridges, dams, skyscrapers, and what we may call today with the terms such as industry or technology as mentioned كَانُوا أَشَدَّ مِنْهُمْ قُوَّةً وَأَثَارُوا الْأَرْضَ وَعَمَرُوهَا أَكْثَرَ مِمَّا عَمَرُوهَا.

---

174. Say, [O Muhammad], "Have you considered that which you invoke besides Allah? Show me what they have created of the earth; or did they have partnership in [creation of] the heavens? Bring me a scripture [revealed] before this or a [remaining] trace of knowledge, if you should be truthful."

175. Have they not traveled through the earth and observed how was the end of those before them? They were greater than them in power, and they plowed the earth and built it up more than they have built it up, and their messengers came to them with clear evidences. And Allah would not ever have wronged them, but they were wronging themselves. Have they not traveled through the land and observed how was the end of those before them? They were more numerous than themselves and greater in strength and in impression on the land, but they were not availed by what they used to earn.

One can realize these deep and void struggles sometimes can be destroyed and terminated due to their open and belligerent attitudes as mentioned [176] in أَوَ لَمْ يَسِيرُوا فِي الْأَرْضِ فَيَنظُرُوا كَيْفَ كَانَ عَاقِبَةُ فَأَخَذَهُمُ اللَّهُ بِذُنُوبِهِمْ الَّذِينَ كَانُوا مِن قَبْلِهِمْ كَانُوا هُمْ أَشَدَّ مِنْهُمْ قُوَّةً وَآثَارًا فِي الْأَرْضِ فَأَخَذَهُمُ اللَّهُ بِذُنُوبِهِمْ وَمَا كَانَ لَهُم مِّنَ اللَّهِ مِن وَاقٍ {غافر/12}. May Allah ﷻ, protect us, Amìn.

The Blind Followers of Āthār

إِنَّهُمْ أَلْفَوْا آبَاءهُمْ ضَالِّينَ {الصافات/69} فَهُمْ عَلَى آثَارِهِمْ يُهْرَعُونَ {الصافات/70} وَلَقَدْ ضَلَّ قَبْلَهُمْ أَكْثَرُ الْأَوَّلِينَ [177] {الصافات/71}

One can realize there are always individuals or people who would follow their society, culture, forefathers, parents or norms blindly. They would not critically think. They would consider thinking and analyzing their inherited norms or teachings as a problem. When they were asked they were explicitly and open declare this disposition as [178] بَلْ قَالُوا إِنَّا وَجَدْنَا آبَاءنَا عَلَى أُمَّةٍ وَإِنَّا عَلَى آثَارِهِم مُّهْتَدُونَ {الزخرف/22}

وَكَذَلِكَ مَا أَرْسَلْنَا مِن قَبْلِكَ فِي قَرْيَةٍ مِّن نَّذِيرٍ إِلَّا قَالَ مُتْرَفُوهَا إِنَّا وَجَدْنَا آبَاءنَا عَلَى أُمَّةٍ وَإِنَّا عَلَى آثَارِهِم مُّقْتَدُونَ {الزخرف/23}

Āthār of Rahmah of Allah ﷻ

فَانظُرْ إِلَى آثَارِ رَحْمَتِ اللَّهِ كَيْفَ يُحْيِي الْأَرْضَ بَعْدَ مَوْتِهَا إِنَّ ذَلِكَ لَمُحْيِي الْمَوْتَى وَهُوَ عَلَى كُلِّ شَيْءٍ قَدِيرٌ [179] {الروم/50}

When we look all the creation, everything is āthār of Allah ﷻ. Yet, the ayah wants us to focus the āthār of Rahmah, Fadl and Grace of Allah ﷻ. In this regard, one can realize that our creation is with the Rahmah of Allah ﷻ. Our recreation in the afterlife is also with the Rahmah of Allah ﷻ.

---

176. Have they not traveled through the land and observed how was the end of those who were before them? They were greater than them in strength and in impression on the land, but Allah seized them for their sins. And they had not from Allah any protector.
177. Indeed they found their fathers astray. So they hastened [to follow] in their footsteps. And there had already strayed before them most of the former peoples,
178. Rather, they say, "Indeed, we found our fathers upon a religion, and we are in their footsteps [rightly] guided." And similarly, We did not send before you any warner into a city except that its affluent said, "Indeed, we found our fathers upon a religion, and we are, in their footsteps, following."
179. So observe the effects of the mercy of Allah—how He gives life to the earth after its lifelessness. Indeed, that [same one] will give life to the dead, and He is over all things competent.

In other words, our existence is with the Rahmah of Allah ﷻ. There is no requirement for Allah ﷻ to create us and to make us existent. Therefore, it is rude, and is the belligerent attitude of kufr when people think, claim or act in the dispositions of ungratefulness. In other words, if we are existence with the Fadl and Rahmah of Allah ﷻ, then this requires always the embodiment of gratitude and shukr to Allah ﷻ.

Not recognizing Allah ﷻ explicitly or implicitly is the full rude and belligerent attitude of evil. Blaming evil on destiny or qadar with the popular notions of theodicy are another form of rude and belligerent attitude of ungratefulness. One should always ask easiness in life from Allah ﷻ as mentioned by Rasulullah ﷺ. This is different. Yet, all the evil-seeming incidents come to a person as a gentle reminder to re-adjust their belligerent and rude attitude with their Rabb, ﷻ.

At another perspective, due to this Rahmah and Fadl of Allah ﷻ, Allah ﷻ recreates us in the afterlife as mentioned فَانْظُرْ إِلَى آثَارِ رَحْمَتِ اللَّهِ كَيْفَ يُحْيِي الْأَرْضَ بَعْدَ مَوْتِهَا إِنَّ ذَلِكَ لَمُحْيِي الْمَوْتَى. On top of it, Allah ﷻ, gives us an eternal life with the Divine Rahmah and Fadl as we humans still not appreciate Allah ﷻ as mentioned [180] وَمَا قَدَرُوا اللَّهَ حَقَّ قَدْرِهِ وَالْأَرْضُ جَمِيعًا قَبْضَتُهُ يَوْمَ الْقِيَامَةِ وَالسَّمَاوَاتُ مَطْوِيَّاتٌ بِيَمِينِهِ سُبْحَانَهُ وَتَعَالَى عَمَّا يُشْرِكُونَ {الزمر/76}.

اَللَّهم جعلنا مِن الشاكِرين

Allahumma Ja'alna min ashhakirìn

اللهم جعلنا من التوابين

Allahumma Ja'alna min attawwābìn

اللهم جعلنا من اتبع اثرك و اثر رسولك ﷺ

Allahumma Ja'alna man attiba' atharaKa wa athāra Rasululuk ﷺ

Juz 26

Sûrah 49 al-Fath

[29]

مُحَمَّدٌ رَّسُولُ اللَّهِ وَالَّذِينَ مَعَهُ أَشِدَّاء عَلَى الْكُفَّارِ رُحَمَاء بَيْنَهُمْ تَرَاهُمْ رُكَّعًا سُجَّدًا يَبْتَغُونَ فَضْلًا مِّنَ اللَّهِ وَرِضْوَانًا سِيمَاهُمْ فِي وُجُوهِهِم مِّنْ أَثَرِ السُّجُودِ ذَلِكَ مَثَلُهُمْ فِي التَّوْرَاةِ وَمَثَلُهُمْ فِي الْإِنجِيلِ كَزَرْعٍ أَخْرَجَ شَطْأَهُ فَآزَرَهُ فَاسْتَغْلَظَ فَاسْتَوَى عَلَى سُوقِهِ يُعْجِبُ

---

180. They have not appraised Allah with true appraisal, while the earth entirely will be [within] His grip on the Day of Resurrection, and the heavens will be folded in His right hand. Exalted is He and high above what they associate with Him.

الزُّرَّاعَ لِيَغِيظَ بِهِمُ الْكُفَّارَ وَعَدَ اللَّهُ الَّذِينَ آمَنُوا وَعَمِلُوا الصَّالِحَاتِ مِنْهُم مَّغْفِرَةً وَأَجْرًا عَظِيمًا [181] {الفتح/29}.

Pride

As we change our terminologies in the need of changing times and culture, pride can have positive meaning at our times compared to the classical and traditional understandings.

In this regard, the word pride can especially reflect our positive identity in our relation with Islām as being a Muslim. This is mentioned in the Qurān as مُحَمَّدٌ رَّسُولُ اللَّهِ in مُحَمَّدٌ رَّسُولُ اللَّهِ وَالَّذِينَ مَعَهُ أَشِدَّاء عَلَى الْكُفَّارِ وَالَّذِينَ مَعَهُ أَشِدَّاء عَلَى الْكُفَّارِ رُحَمَاء بَيْنَهُمْ تَرَاهُمْ رُكَّعًا سُجَّدًا يَبْتَغُونَ فَضْلًا مِّنَ اللَّهِ وَرِضْوَانًا سِيمَاهُمْ فِي وُجُوهِهِم مِّنْ أَثَرِ السُّجُودِ ذَلِكَ مَثَلُهُمْ فِي التَّوْرَاةِ وَمَثَلُهُمْ فِي الْإِنجِيلِ كَزَرْعٍ أَخْرَجَ شَطْأَهُ فَآزَرَهُ فَاسْتَغْلَظَ فَاسْتَوَى عَلَى سُوقِهِ يُعْجِبُ الزُّرَّاعَ لِيَغِيظَ بِهِمُ الْكُفَّارَ وَعَدَ اللَّهُ الَّذِينَ آمَنُوا وَعَمِلُوا الصَّالِحَاتِ مِنْهُم مَّغْفِرَةً وَأَجْرًا عَظِيمًا {الفتح/29}.

As a Muslim especially compared to other group associations, Allah ﷻ bestowed us the ni'mah of the Qurān and Rasulullah ﷺ. Being proud of this ni'mah and also being in full appreciation and gratitutude to Allah ﷻ is very critical.

Yet, when we review the concept of pride, we don't mean the notions of superior group related identities that make the person or people defend a team similar to the fans of a soccer or other sports.

More than external, we mean the internal stance of pride, confidence, certainty, conviction and self-assurance about our identity as a Muslim.

This can reveal itself in our social engagements especially with non-Muslims in the display of pride, confidence and assurance for our gratitude and appreciation of this enormous n'imah to Allah ﷻ.

---

181. Muhammad is the Messenger of Allah; and those with him are forceful against the disbelievers, merciful among themselves. You see them bowing and prostrating [in prayer], seeking bounty from Allah and [His] pleasure. Their mark is on their faces from the trace of prostration. That is their description in the Torah. And their description in the Gospel is as a plant which produces its offshoots and strengthens them so they grow firm and stand upon their stalks, delighting the sowers—so that Allah may enrage by them the disbelievers. Allah has promised those who believe and do righteous deeds among them forgiveness and a great reward.

In this regard, all our mann, appreciation and thanking is to Allah ﷺ as mentioned [182] يَمُنُّونَ عَلَيْكَ أَنْ أَسْلَمُوا قُل لاَّ تَمُنُّوا عَلَيَّ إِسْلاَمَكُم بَلِ اللَّهُ يَمُنُّ عَلَيْكُمْ أَنْ هَدَاكُمْ لِلْإِيمَانِ إِن كُنتُمْ صَادِقِينَ {الحجرات/17}.

When we meet and constantly see people who do not have any substantial teaching and yet, they popularize them with their limited, incomplete and inconsistent content, can display attitudes of pride in them.

Yet, as we have the full and flawless teachings from Allah ﷺ through the Qurān and Rasulullah ﷺ, our intimate and shy approaches can be inappropriacy where the notions of pride and confidence can be more befitting manners of the heart and mind in our display of gratitude to Allah ﷺ.

One should remember that this approach referred as pride should be especially present in our relationships with the ones who are not Muslims.

A Muslim is expected to display of leniency with their other Muslim fellows as mentioned رُحَمَاء بَيْنَهُمْ at all times. Allahu A'lam.

Sûrah 49 al-Hujurāt

[13]

The Purpose of Gender and Ethnicity Differences

يَا أَيُّهَا النَّاسُ إِنَّا خَلَقْنَاكُم مِّن ذَكَرٍ وَأُنثَى وَجَعَلْنَاكُمْ شُعُوبًا وَقَبَائِلَ لِتَعَارَفُوا إِنَّ أَكْرَمَكُمْ عِندَ اللَّهِ أَتْقَاكُمْ إِنَّ اللَّهَ عَلِيمٌ خَبِيرٌ [183] {الحجرات/13}

It is interesting to realize that Allah ﷺ created men and women to know each other if one can read the ayah as لِتَعَارَفُوا إِنَّا خَلَقْنَاكُم مِّن ذَكَرٍ وَأُنثَى.

In this regard, it is important understand and study gender, femininity and masculinity. The expression لِتَعَارَفُوا can indicate knowing and understanding one's differences through gender.

---

182. They consider it a favor to you that they have accepted Islam. Say, "Do not consider your Islam a favor to me. Rather, Allah has conferred favor upon you that He has guided you to the faith, if you should be truthful."

183. O mankind, indeed We have created you from male and female and made you peoples and tribes that you may know one another. Indeed, the most noble of you in the sight of Allah is the most righteous of you. Indeed, Allah is Knowing and Acquainted.

In the understanding of these differences as displayed through gender, one of the focus can be in the interaction and differences between husband and wife in a marriage.

When a person accepts and tries to recognize these differences in genders between husband and wife, one can actually realize that this is one of the ayahs, signs and spiritual openings that can lead the person to the true imān with certainty, yaqìn, and marifatullah. This is mentioned as [184] وَمِنْ آيَاتِهِ أَنْ خَلَقَ لَكُم مِّنْ أَنفُسِكُمْ أَزْوَاجًا لِّتَسْكُنُوا إِلَيْهَا وَجَعَلَ بَيْنَكُم مَّوَدَّةً وَرَحْمَةً إِنَّ فِي ذَلِكَ لَآيَاتٍ لِّقَوْمٍ يَتَفَكَّرُونَ {الروم/21}.

The phrase وَمِنْ آيَاتِهِ as repeated in Sûrah Rûm can indicate these signs of Allah ﷻ for one's imān. In this case, the sign is one's difference through gender correspondence between man and woman.

Similarly, when we combine this teaching of differences through culture, color, and ethnicity, the ayah also includes وَجَعَلْنَاكُمْ شُعُوبًا وَقَبَائِلَ لِتَعَارَفُوا. In other words, other than gender differences, differences related with culture, ethnicity or race can be realized, recognized and studied.

In this regard, Allah ﷻ mentions in Sûrah Rûm that this is also one of the ayahs, signs and spiritual openings that one can use to increase one's imān with yaqìn in Allah ﷻ as mentioned [185] وَمِنْ آيَاتِهِ خَلْقُ السَّمَاوَاتِ وَالْأَرْضِ وَاخْتِلَافُ أَلْسِنَتِكُمْ وَأَلْوَانِكُمْ إِنَّ فِي ذَلِكَ لَآيَاتٍ لِّلْعَالِمِينَ {الروم/22}.

In this regard, the expression وَاخْتِلَافُ أَلْسِنَتِكُمْ وَأَلْوَانِكُمْ specifically underlines this as one of the ayahs of Allah ﷻ.

Studying, recognizing and accepting all these differences can lead to the true imān with yaqìn in Allah ﷻ. Accordingly, the ranking or superiority among them does not display due to the humanly pseudo-rankings valuing or devaluing the genders, races or ethnicities. The true ranking is with one's real proximity to Allah ﷻ in their relationship as mentioned إِنَّ أَكْرَمَكُمْ عِندَ اللَّهِ أَتْقَاكُمْ.

Since Allah ﷻ is only the One Who knows a person's true proximity with Allah ﷻ as mentioned إِنَّ اللَّهَ عَلِيمٌ خَبِيرٌ, therefore no one can has the right, awareness, and knowledge to judge another in their humanly social engagements of this world.

---

184. And of His signs is that He created for you from yourselves mates that you may find tranquillity in them; and He placed between you affection and mercy. Indeed in that are signs for a people who give thought.

185. And of His signs is the creation of the heavens and the earth and the diversity of your languages and your colors. Indeed in that are signs for those of knowledge.

Harmonizing Differences

When we analyze the Qurān to focus on the differences in the creation of Allah ☀, one can realize that Allah ☀ has created and assigned responsibilities to the beings, and natural events harmonizing, balancing and completing each other with their differences.

One can realize this with the key repeated term of these apparent but harmonizing differences in the Qurān with اختلاف.

There is a harmonizing and balancing difference in the change of day and night as mentioned [186]

وَاخْتِلَافِ اللَّيْلِ وَالنَّهَارِ وَمَا أَنزَلَ اللهُ مِنَ السَّمَاء مِن رِّزْقٍ فَأَحْيَا بِهِ الْأَرْضَ بَعْدَ مَوْتِهَا وَتَصْرِيفِ الرِّيَاحِ آيَاتٌ لِّقَوْمٍ يَعْقِلُونَ {الجاثية/5}

إِنَّ فِي خَلْقِ السَّمَاوَاتِ وَالْأَرْضِ وَاخْتِلَافِ اللَّيْلِ وَالنَّهَارِ وَالْفُلْكِ الَّتِي تَجْرِي فِي الْبَحْرِ بِمَا يَنفَعُ النَّاسَ وَمَا أَنزَلَ اللهُ مِنَ السَّمَاء مِن مَّاء فَأَحْيَا بِهِ الْأَرْضَ بَعْدَ مَوْتِهَا وَبَثَّ فِيهَا مِن كُلِّ دَابَّةٍ وَتَصْرِيفِ الرِّيَاحِ وَالسَّحَابِ الْمُسَخِّرِ بَيْنَ السَّمَاء وَالأَرْضِ لآيَاتٍ لِّقَوْمٍ يَعْقِلُونَ {البقرة/164}

إِنَّ فِي خَلْقِ السَّمَاوَاتِ وَالأَرْضِ وَاخْتِلاَفِ اللَّيْلِ وَالنَّهَارِ لآيَاتٍ لِّأُوْلِي الألْبَابِ {آل عمران/190}

وَهُوَ الَّذِي يُحْيِي وَيُمِيتُ وَلَهُ اخْتِلَافُ اللَّيْلِ وَالنَّهَارِ أَفَلَا تَعْقِلُونَ {المؤمنون/80}

There is a harmonizing and balancing difference in the change of the different economic and financial levels among people as mentioned in the above ayah as وَمَا أَنزَلَ اللهُ مِنَ السَّمَاء مِن رِّزْقٍ.

In all of these harmonizing and balancing differences, there is a sign for the people critical thinking, intellect and for the people of logic

---

186. And [in] the alternation of night and day and [in] what Allah sends down from the sky of provision and gives life thereby to the earth after its lifelessness and [in His] directing of the winds are signs for a people who reason. Indeed, the creation of the heavens and earth, and the alternation of the night and the day, and the [great] ships which sail through the sea with that which benefits people, and what Allah has sent down from the heavens of rain, giving life thereby to the earth after its lifelessness and dispersing therein every [kind of] moving creature, and [His] directing of the winds and the clouds controlled between the heaven and the earth are signs for a people who use reason. Indeed, in the creation of the heavens and the earth and the alternation of the night and the day are signs for those of understanding. And it is He who gives life and causes death, and His is the alternation of the night and the day. Then will you not reason?

آيَاتٌ لِّقَوْمٍ يَعْقِلُونَ {الجاثية/5}, لآيَاتٍ لِّقَوْمٍ يَعْقِلُونَ [187] as repeatedly mentioned as {البقرة/164}, لآيَاتٍ لِّأُوْلِي الْأَلْبَابِ {آل عمران/190}, أَفَلَا تَعْقِلُونَ {المؤمنون/80}

Yet, one should remember that the effect of the embodiment of these signs should lead the person from knowing, understanding, and realizing into the higher level of acting which is called taqwa. If one recognizes these signs but still maintains carelessness and heedless, then this knowledge will not extend more than an intellectual engagement.

Yet, the true knowledge of a person should change the person with these teachings or signs. This is called taqwa. This is mentioned as [188] إِنَّ فِي اخْتِلَافِ اللَّيْلِ وَالنَّهَارِ وَمَا خَلَقَ اللَّهُ فِي السَّمَاوَاتِ وَالأَرْضِ لآيَاتٍ لِّقَوْمٍ يَتَّقُونَ {يونس/6}

One should remember that the opposites in their apparent and external forms are not evil, not competing with each other and are not opponent of each other. In reality, they are all helping each other to form unity, balance, perfection of one another. In physics, the terms positron and electron annihilation can show this unity in the material world with an emission of photon [14].

In the concepts and terminologies of religion, the darkness and pessimistic states of kufr leading to chaos in personal lives can make the person find, realize, understand and excel in the positive valleys of imān.

In this regard, any type of engagement that disconnect the person, ideas and thoughts from Allah ﷻ is kufr. Imān is the effort taking a meaning from its external or apparent meanings into the real meanings in their relationships with Allah ﷻ. Therefore, Jahannam is a fruit of kufr. Jannah is a fruit of imān. Kufr is a seed. Imān is a seed.

A person in their lifelong struggle of imān gets the fruit of Jannah to eat, enjoy and be with Allah ﷻ without any diseases and frictions of the nafs and Shaytān in Jannah.

---

187. And [in] the alternation of night and day and [in] what Allah sends down from the sky of provision and gives life thereby to the earth after its lifelessness and [in His] directing of the winds are signs for a people who reason. And it is He who gives life and causes death, and His is the alternation of the night and the day. Then will you not reason? Indeed, in the creation of the heavens and the earth and the alternation of the night and the day are signs for those of understanding. Indeed, in the creation of the heavens and earth, and the alternation of the night and the day, and the [great] ships which sail through the sea with that which benefits people, and what Allah has sent down from the heavens of rain, giving life thereby to the earth after its lifelessness and dispersing therein every [kind of] moving creature, and [His] directing of the winds and the clouds controlled between the heaven and the earth are signs for a people who use reason.

188. Indeed, in the alternation of the night and the day and [in] what Allah has created in the heavens and the earth are signs for a people who fear Allah

A person in their lifelong struggle of kufr gets the fruit of Jahannam to suffer further without Allah ﷻ in Jahannam with Shaytān, and his or her friends who has the lowly nafs (nafs ammarah).

"Everyone will be whom they love" is a hadith [4] that also supports this stance.

Differences & Temporality

أَفَلاَ يَتَدَبَّرُونَ الْقُرْآنَ وَلَوْ كَانَ مِنْ عِندِ غَيْرِ اللّهِ لَوَجَدُواْ فِيهِ اخْتِلاَفًا كَثِيرًا 189 {النساء/82}

One should remember that change indicates temporality. All the temporals have differences, and changes.

Allah ﷻ is al-Baki and al-Qayyum, the Infinite and the Permanent. Anything related with Allah ﷻ can have these attributes with the permission and enablement of Allah ﷻ as mentioned مَن ذَا الَّذِي يَشْفَعُ عِنْدَهُ إِلاَّ بِإِذْنِهِ and وَلاَ يُحِيطُونَ بِشَيْءٍ مِّنْ عِلْمِهِ إِلاَّ بِمَا شَاء. The Qurān is the Kalamullah. There is no change and difference in the Qurān as mentioned أَفَلاَ يَتَدَبَّرُونَ الْقُرْآنَ وَلَوْ كَانَ مِنْ عِندِ غَيْرِ اللّهِ لَوَجَدُواْ فِيهِ اخْتِلاَفًا كَثِيرًا {النساء/82}. Therefore, the Qurān is sufficient to prove that the Qurān is from Allah ﷻ and Kalamullah.

Depending on their proximity with Allah ﷻ, Allah ﷻ can bestow some of these qualities on the creation, a'bd.

One of the examples of this can be Jibril as among angels as referred as Ruhul Qudus. Jibril as has special uniqueness in terms of delivery the Wahiy and giving life with the permission, enablement and proximity to Allah ﷻ as one of the highest ab'dullah.

Another example of this can be Rasulullah ﷺ among humans and even among entire creation. It is mentioned in different narrations Adam as made tawbah with Allah ﷻ when he as observed the phrase at the door of Jannah written as "La ilaha illa Allah Muhammadan Rasulullah" [6]. Another example to prove the high proximity of Rasulullah ﷺ to Allah ﷻ is the case of all creation in the Judgment Day. No one can dare to talk or even move except Rasulullah ﷺ [4].

Allahumma Ja'alna Tabi'u Rasulullah ﷺ, Amīn!

---

189. Then do they not reflect upon the Qurán? If it had been from [any] other than Allah, they would have found within it much contradiction.

Juz 27

Sûrah 55 -Al-Rahmãn

[16]

{الرحمن/16} 190 فَبِأَيِّ آلَاء رَبِّكُمَا تُكَذِّبَانِ

When we ponder upon the hikmah of the thirty-one times repetition of the above ayah in this short Sûrah, one can deduce some realities about humans.

First, humans have tendency to engage themselves with theodicy as much popularized today. Theodicy is a term when the person engages themselves with negative attitudes of expectation from Allah ﷻ. In this regard, due to the loss of adab with Allah ﷻ, the expressions of "blaming God" becomes a normal talk. This critical ayah addresses this human reality of theodicy in their relationship with Allah ﷻ. How can a person have a negative relation or expectation from Allah ﷻ after all these are mentioned and repeated in this Sûrah?

Second, humans do not appreciate what Allah ﷻ gives to them constantly. Humans have the disease of being ungrateful. In this regard, disbelief, kufr is a term for a person who does not appreciate but cover the things up. This repetition of this ayah in this Sûrah constantly reminds us this nature of humans that we are not grateful. If we were, then there would not need to have any repetition. Since there is a repetition, that means that we are not grateful as mentioned إِنَّ الْإِنسَانَ 191 وَقَلِيلٌ مِّنْ عِبَادِيَ الشَّكُورُ {سبأ/13} and لِرَبِّهِ لَكَنُودٌ {العاديات/6}.

Third, humans constantly forget these realities that need appreciation, therefore, they need to be constantly reminded by repetition. We forget as our species name in Arabic is al-insãn, the one who forgets. The reality of repetition of this ayah reminds us the need for constant reminders of Allah ﷻ in order to maintain some level of appreciation and gratefulness to Allah ﷻ. This constant reminder for Allah ﷻ is called Dhikrullah. In its absolute sense, the Qurãn is the prime Dhikrullah. Rasulullah, the sunnah and the hadith is the essential Dhikrullah to know how to

---

190. So which of the favors of your Lord would you deny ?
191. They made for him what he willed of elevated chambers, statues, bowls like reservoirs, and stationary kettles. [We said], "Work, O family of David, in gratitude." And few of My servants are grateful. Indeed mankind, to his Lord, is ungrateful.

implement the primary source, the Qurãn. Other forms of reminders as Dhikrullah can be anything or incident that is constantly showering on us in our individual lives. A trial, a test, an animal, an ant, a breeze, a look, a sound, a death, a thought can be all different forms ayahs or signs remind the person for Dhikrullah as mentioned [192] سَنُرِيهِمْ آيَاتِنَا فِي الْأَفَاقِ .وَفِي أَنفُسِهِمْ حَتَّى يَتَبَيَّنَ لَهُمْ أَنَّهُ الْحَقُّ أَوَلَمْ يَكْفِ بِرَبِّكَ أَنَّهُ عَلَى كُلِّ شَيْءٍ شَهِيدٌ {فصلت/53}

Juz 28

Sûrah 63 – al- Munafiqûn

[7]

هُمُ الَّذِينَ يَقُولُونَ لَا تُنفِقُوا عَلَى مَنْ عِندَ رَسُولِ اللَّهِ حَتَّى يَنفَضُّوا وَلِلَّهِ خَزَائِنُ السَّمَاوَاتِ وَالْأَرْضِ وَلَكِنَّ الْمُنَافِقِينَ لَا يَفْقَهُونَ [193] {المنافقون/7}

One of the attributes of nifãq is to block, prevent, and discourage people from doing khayr, virtuous and good actions or engagements. This is also explicitly mentioned in [194] مَنَّاعٍ لِّلْخَيْرِ مُعْتَدٍ أَثِيمٍ {القلم/12}. One should really check their heart and mind if there is khayr that does not belong to him or her or their group, family and identity, do we still encourage it? Or, do we implicitly or explicitly engage in emotions, conversations or even actions, May Allah ﷻ protect us, to prevent it or discourage people doing it?

Astagfirullah, our spiritual diseases are far more than our physical diseases. Yet, people shut down the world due to a pandemic virus. Yet, we have the pandemic disease of arrogance, hasad, zulm, oppression, abuse, and other many deadly ones. No one cares about them and assumes that they don't exist or they are not a big deal.

Allah ﷻ takes care of all universe, galaxy, micro and macro worlds in their maintance of the ecosystem. So, really our position should not be the material diseases or material world starting with our physical bodies with physical health concerns and other related ones. Our real

---

192. We will show them Our signs in the horizons and within themselves until it becomes clear to them that it is the truth. But is it not sufficient concerning your Lord that He is, over all things, a Witness?
193. They are the ones who say, "Do not spend on those who are with the Messenger of Allah until they disband." And to Allah belongs the depositories of the heavens and the earth, but the hypocrites do not understand.
194. A preventer of good, transgressing and sinful,

concern should be to focus, prevent and cure our spiritual diseases in this short life before it is too late. We will be primarily responsible in front of Allah ﷺ for our struggle against our spiritual diseases but not physical externalities.

Juz 30

Sûrah 109 al-Kafirûn, Sûrah 112 al-Ikhlas, Sûrah 113 al-Falaq & Sûrah 114 an-Nâs

بِسْمِ اللهِ الرَّحْمَنِ الرَّحِيمِ

قُلْ يَا أَيُّهَا الْكَافِرُونَ {الكافرون/1} لَا أَعْبُدُ مَا تَعْبُدُونَ {الكافرون/2} وَلَا أَنتُمْ عَابِدُونَ مَا أَعْبُدُ 195 {الكافرون/3} وَلَا أَنَا عَابِدٌ مَّا عَبَدتُّمْ {الكافرون/4} وَلَا أَنتُمْ عَابِدُونَ مَا أَعْبُدُ {الكافرون/5} لَكُمْ دِينُكُمْ وَلِيَ دِينِ {الكافرون/6}

بِسْمِ اللهِ الرَّحْمَنِ الرَّحِيمِ

قُلْ هُوَ اللهُ أَحَدٌ {الإخلاص/1} اللهُ الصَّمَدُ {الإخلاص/2} لَمْ يَلِدْ وَلَمْ يُولَدْ {الإخلاص/3} وَلَمْ يَكُن لَّهُ كُفُوًا أَحَدٌ {الإخلاص/4}

بِسْمِ اللهِ الرَّحْمَنِ الرَّحِيمِ

قُلْ أَعُوذُ بِرَبِّ الْفَلَقِ {الفلق/1} مِن شَرِّ مَا خَلَقَ {الفلق/2} وَمِن شَرِّ غَاسِقٍ إِذَا وَقَبَ {الفلق/3} وَمِن شَرِّ النَّفَّاثَاتِ فِي الْعُقَدِ {الفلق/4} وَمِن شَرِّ حَاسِدٍ إِذَا حَسَدَ {الفلق/5}

بِسْمِ اللهِ الرَّحْمَنِ الرَّحِيمِ

قُلْ أَعُوذُ بِرَبِّ النَّاسِ {الناس/1} مَلِكِ النَّاسِ {الناس/2} إِلَهِ النَّاسِ {الناس/3} مِن شَرِّ الْوَسْوَاسِ الْخَنَّاسِ {الناس/4} الَّذِي يُوَسْوِسُ فِي صُدُورِ النَّاسِ {الناس/5} مِنَ الْجِنَّةِ وَ النَّاسِ {الناس/6}

---

195. Say, "O disbelievers, I do not worship what you worship. Nor are you worshippers of what I worship. Nor will I be a worshipper of what you worship. Nor will you be worshippers of what I worship. For you is your religion, and for me is my religion." Say, "He is Allah, [who is] One, Allah, the Eternal Refuge. He neither begets nor is born, Nor is there to Him any equivalent." Say, "I seek refuge in the Lord of daybreak From the evil of that which He created And from the evil of darkness when it settles And from the evil of the blowers in knots And from the evil of an envier when he envies."Say, "I seek refuge in the Lord of mankind, The Sovereign of mankind. From the evil of the retreating whisperer—Who whispers [evil] into the breasts of mankind—From among the jinn and mankind."

Rasulullah ﷺ read above four Sûrahs read at different times in different prayers and for different virtues.

For example, it is sunnah to read Sûrah al-kafirûn and al-ikhlas both in fajr and magrib sunnahs [7].

It is sunnah to read Sûrahs al-Ikhlas, al-Falaq and al-Nãs for protection purposes in the morning, at night and before sleep thrice [6] [16].

Reading Sûrah ikhlas thrice is similar to the virtue of reading the one third of the Qurãn [17].

One of the common words and symmetrical positions of all four Sûrahs is that they also start with the phrase of order of قُل.

This phrase قُل itself is a sufficient proof for the true prophet of Rasulullah ﷺ and the authenticity of the Qurãn.

The phrase قُل clearly declares that Rasulullah ﷺ as a human and ab'd of Allah ﷻ delivers the message to humans.

Uluhiyyah & Sûrah Ikhlas

The phrase قُل clearly declares that the true uluhiyyah of Allah ﷻ should be given and instructed as an inductive teaching by Allah ﷻ to humans about the Divine Dhãt as mentioned especially in Sûrah Ikhlãs. One can deduce and prove the elements of teachings in Sûrah ikhlas. Yet, to confirm the mind, the inductive teachings should be by wahiy, revelation from Allah SWT about the Transcendent Reality of Allah ﷻ so that there is no improper approximations as some others such as Christians did with the concept of trinity. Since humans are limited, Allah ﷻ is al-Bakì. The true knowledge about the Dhãt of Allah ﷻ, uluhiyyah should be given as an inductive, top-down approach of wahiy to humans. Humans can approximate meanings about Allah ﷻ. Yet, these are all approximations unless these approximations are confirmed with the true and absolute knowledge of wahiy, revelation from Allah ﷻ as an inductive teaching.

Limited humans cannot claim to know about Allah ﷻ who is Transcendent, al-Bakì, beyond humans limited approximations. Knowing something can mean comprehending and surrounding that thing mentally, by intellect, logic and mind. Yet, limited humans cannot know truly about Allah ﷻ who is al-Baki, Transcedneted, Unlimited and

Infinite unless with the permissibility of this true knowledge given by
Allah ☙ as mentioned شَاء بِمَا إِلاَّ عِلْمِهِ مِّنْ بِشَيْءٍ يُحيطُونَ وَلاَ.

If take the example of trinity in Christianity, if one reviews the
current Bible, there is no place in the Bible that clearly or explicitly
mentions about the trinity once. Even if the current bible is the one
which is distorted, not original, as also acknowledged by Christian
scholarship [18]. Then, one can ask if trinity is the basis of the creed in
Christianity why the Bible as a revelation from God would not mention
this critical and essential creed in the sacred revelation? In this regard,
Jewish scholarship asks the same question to Christian scholarship. In
this sense, the understanding of tawhid is similar in Islām and Judaism.

On the other hand, if we review the Qurān and hadith, there are
hundreds of places in the Qurān and hadith that explicitly mentions and
explains about the tawhid, the true uluhiyyah of Allah ☙. One can even
only review the ayahs of the Qurān with the phrases such as "Allahu
La ilaha illa Huwa, Huwa Allahu Allazi La ilaha illa Huwa, La ilaha
illa Allah" and many others. The true Uluhiyyah of Allah ☙ should be
instructed and given as an inductive teaching in the wahiy, revelation
by Allah ☙. This is another proof about the authenticity and originality
of the Qurān and Rasulullah ☙. The Qurān explicitly mentions about
the Uluhiyyah of Allah ☙ in many places.

The main creed about the Creator cannot be based on secondary,
mystical or interpretative meanings that can lead people illusionary,
unstable discourses of skepticism, agnosticism, spirituality or nones
or others [19]. This is unfortunately a dalalah even people have good
intentions. Yet, there are pillars of the religion such as the knowledge
about Uluhiyyah which should be on clear and simple pillars. This
knowledge should be referenced to the clear inductive teachings of
wahiy, revelation as instructed by Allah ☙.

Unfortuntaely, today's formations of "nones", unstable discourses
of skepticism, spirituality due to a protest against organized or
institutionalized religions are all due to the second wave effects of this
creed problem of trinity in Christianity. Today, Christianity is losing
blood due to a major creed problem although Christianity has many
virtuous, ethical and moral renderings contributing the society in
their service to humanity. I think, if the genuine and sincere Christian
scholarship review their own self accountability of the problems, they
would realize the issue and try to fix it by first acknowledging it and,

then going forward with true tawhid of Allah ﷻ. If not, negative group identities with belongings would hinder not to see their problems and issues, and they would become weak and weaker, and will eventually disappear.

Positive Group Associations & Sûrah Kafirûn

The phrase قُل clearly declares that at the end of the day, there will be group associations as mentioned in Sûrah al-Kafirûn. Yet, a believer of Allah ﷻ and the follower of Rasulullah ﷺ and follower of Isa as, Ibrahim as and Musa as and other prophets as Muslims should clearly mention their disposition at one point but not cross the boundaries of positive group identities of a believer. This especially occurs when people approach everything with possibilities, agnosticism, or skepticism or recent illusionary approaches of religion or cultural appropriations. In this regard, there is an implicit hit on the positive group associations of being a Muslim as the follower of Rasulullah ﷺ on the path of Allah ﷻ by expanding the popular negative discourses against the institutionalized religions. The term institutionalized religion is an implicit term to make the religions fluid with a term called "nones" or "spiritual" [19].

Dynamism in the Universe and Sûrah Falaq

The phrase قُل clearly declares the dynamic discourses of interactions in the universe with the motion or stationary states in micro and macro realms of change of time, light, sunset, sunrise, and all other known and unknown engagements to humans especially with Sûrah Falaq. As humans are always naturally scared of the unknowns. This Sûrah with Sûrah al-Nãs teaches us to ask constant protection and refuge in Allah ﷻ in the causalities of these unknowns to us in the bigger ocean of the qada and qadar of Allah ﷻ.

Humans at the Center of Creation and Sûrah al-Nãs

The phrase قُل clearly declares and reminds us as humans as the center of all creation as mentioned as a closing or final remark in the last Sûrah of the Qurãn in Sûrah al-Nas. The purpose of universe and existence of other creation is humans as the name of this Sûrah is al-Nas. There is a ta'kid and emphasis on humans with their relationsip with Allah ﷻ as: [196]

.إِلَهِ النَّاسِ {3/الناس} and مَلِكِ النَّاسِ {2/الناس} and, بِرَبِّ النَّاسِ {1/الناس}.

The phrase بِرَبِّ النَّاسِ {1/الناس} emphasizes especially the relation of humans with their Rabb, Allah ﷻ in the Rububiyyah of Allah ﷻ especially in this life.

The phrase مَلِكِ النَّاسِ {2/الناس} emphasizes especially the relation of humans with their Mālik, Allah ﷻ in their ubudiyyah of Allah ﷻ from the time of their creation and especially in the akhirah as also mentioned in Sûrah Fatiha as [197] {4/الفاتحة} مَلِكِ يَوْمِ الدِّينِ.

The phrase إِلَهِ النَّاسِ {3/الناس} emphasizes especially the relations of humans with Allah ﷻ in the Uluhiyah of Allah ﷻ at all times, from the time of creation including the beginning times or incidents referred as qawlu bala.

This Sûrah as the last Sûrah of the Qurān reminds humans the purpose and hikmah of our existence on the earth with the initial narrative of Shaytān that there is a being that that is working against our purpose of presence in this world. Therefore, we should not forget these realities of temptations as instigated by our own enemies of shaytan tempering our own ego, nafs, with different and billions of possibilities of tricks.

The only way to be safe is to accept our own weakness in all our life philosophy and run back to Allah ﷻ and take refuge in Allah ﷻ with firār as mentinioned repeated with the phrase [198] {1/الفلق} قُلْ أَعُوذُ بِرَبِّ الْفَلَقِ and قُلْ أَعُوذُ بِرَبِّ النَّاسِ.

The phrase أَعُوذُ is hidden and repeated in the above two Sûrahs with a meaning as below:

---

196. Say, "I seek refuge in the Lord of mankind, The Sovereign of mankind. The God of mankind,
197. Sovereign of the Day of Recompense.
198. Say, "I seek refuge in the Lord of daybreak From the evil of that which He created And from the evil of darkness when it settles And from the evil of the blowers in knots And from the evil of an envier when he envies. Say, "I seek refuge in the Lord of mankind, The Sovereign of mankind. The God of mankind, From the evil of the retreating whisperer—Who whispers [evil] into the breasts of mankind—From among the jinn and mankind."

قُلْ أَعُوذُ بِرَبِّ الْفَلَقِ {الفلق/1} أَعُوذُ مِن شَرِّ مَا خَلَقَ {الفلق/2} وَأَعُوذُ مِن شَرِّ غَاسِقٍ إِذَا وَقَبَ {الفلق/3} و أَعُوذُ مِن شَرِّ النَّفَّاثَاتِ فِي الْعُقَدِ {الفلق/4} و أَعُوذُ مِن شَرِّ حَاسِدٍ إِذَا حَسَدَ {الفلق/5}

قُلْ أَعُوذُ بِرَبِّ النَّاسِ {الناس/1}أَعُوذُ بِ مَلِكِ النَّاسِ {الناس/2}أَعُوذُ بِ إِلَهِ النَّاسِ {الناس/3} أَعُوذُ مِن شَرِّ الْوَسْوَاسِ الْخَنَّاسِ {الناس/4} الَّذِي يُوَسْوِسُ فِي صُدُورِ النَّاسِ {الناس/5} أَعُوذُ مِنَ الْجِنَّةِ وَ النَّاسِ {الناس/6}

SubhanAllah, we need so much protection and taking refuge in Allah ﷻ, yet we are in gaflah!

BIBLIOGRAPHY

[1] E. Gearon, The History and Achievements of the Islamic Golden Age, Teaching Company, LLC, 2016.

[2] U. P. Oxford, "Oxford Dictionaries," 2016. [Online]. Available: http://www.oxforddictionaries.com/us/definition/american_english/. [Accessed 2016].

[3] D. B. Burrell, Towards a Jewish-Christian-Muslim Theology, Wiley, 2011.

[4] M. Razi, Mafatih al-Ghayb known as al-Tafsir al-Kabir, Cairo: Dar Ibya al-Kutub al-Bahiyya, 1172.

[5] H. Baghawi, Tafsir al-Baghawi al-musamma Ma'alim al-tanzil, Bayrut: Dar al-Ma'rifah, 1987.

[6] M. Tirmizi, Jami At-Tirmizi, Dar-us-Salam, 2007.

[7] A. Muslim, Sahih Muslim (translated by Siddiqui, A.), Peace Vision, 1972.

[8] M. Al-Bukhari, The translation of the meanings of Sahih Al-Bukhari, Kazi Publications, 1986.

[9] Sawfatul khilya, Zaman , 1997.

[10] S. Vahide, The Collection of Light, ihlas nur publication, 2001.

[11] I. Qusayhri, Tafsirul Qusayhri.

[12] M. i. A. Hakim, Al-Mustadrak: `ala al-sahihayn, Dar al-Kutub al-`Ilmiyyah, 1990, p. 1/612.

[13] M. b. A. b. M. al-Shawkani, Fath ul Qadeer, Lebanon: Dar Al-Fikr Beirut.

[14] Y. Kumek, Ethnographic Field Notes, 2017.

[15] J. W. R. R. David Halliday, Fundamentals of Physics, Wiley, 2013, p. 622.

[16] Q. Iyad, Ash-Shifa, Madina Press, 2006.

[17] S. Abu-Dawud, Sunan Abu Dawud, Riyadh: Darussalam, 2008.

[18] B. D. Ehrman, Misquoting Jesus The Story Behind Who Changed the Bible and Why, HarperOne, 2009.

[19] K. a. Y. Roberts, Religion in Sociological Perspective. 6th edition. 2017, Sage Publishing, 2017, p. 50.

AUTHOR BIO

Dr. Kumek had classical training in Islamic sciences from the respected Shuyûqh/Teachers of Turkey, India, Egypt, Yemen, Somalia, Morocco, Sudan, and the United States. He stayed and studied classical Islamic sciences in Egypt and Turkey as well.

In his Western training, education and teaching experience, Dr. Kumek has acted as the religious studies coordinator at State University of New York (SUNY) Buffalo State and taught undergraduate and graduate courses in religious studies at SUNY at Buffalo State, Niagara University, Daemen College and Harvard Divinity School. Dr. Kumek also pursued doctorate degree in physics at SUNY at Buffalo published academic papers in the areas of quantum physics and medical physics. Then, he decided to engage with the world of social sciences through social anthropology, education, and cultural anthropology in his doctorate studies and subsequently, spent a few years as a research associate in the anthropology department of the same university and subsequently, completed a postdoctoral fellowship at Harvard Divinity school. Some of his book titles include sociology through religion, religious literacy through ethnography, selected passages from the Qurãn, selected passages from the Hadith (titled as Rasulullah ﷺ) and selected prayers of the Prophet Muhammad ﷺ (titled as Pearls and Diamonds). Dr. M. Yunus Kumek is currently teaching on Muslim Ministry and Spiritual Care at Harvard Divinity School.

ACKNOWLEDGMENTS

I would like to thank all my unnamed teachers, friends, and students for their input, ideas, suggestions, help, and support during and before the preparation of this book.

I would like to thank Dr. David Banks, faculty of the Department of Anthropology, State University of New York (SUNY), Sister Toni Hajdaj, Sister Umm Aisha, Dr. AbdulAhad, Br. Ali Rifat and His wife Sister Yildiz at-Turki, Sheikh Dr. Omar of Maryland al-Hindi, Sheikh Tamer of Buffalo, and Sheikh Ali of Hartford Seminary, Sisters Asya Hamad, Amina Osman, and Fatima Samrodia of Darul-Ulum Madania of Buffalo for all their editing, suggestions and comments.

I want to also thank the team of Medina House Publishing in all their preparations and efforts at all stages of this book especially Br. Murat, Br. Khalid (Halit), Br. Mehmet (Matt) and Sister Karen.

Lastly, I would like to thank all of my family members for their patience with me during the preparation of this book.

We ask Allah ﷻ to accept all our efforts with the Divine Karam, Fadl, and Grace but not with our faulty and limited efforts deeming rejection.
اللَّهُمَّ صلِّ عَلى سَيِّدِناَ وَ حَبِيْبَنَا وَ مَوْلَانَا مُحَمَّد.

INDEX